Endorsements for Kugel, Chaos & Unconditional Love

"A touch of humor, a lot of faith,
and stories that make you think.
Chana Gittle Deray's stories add a bit of sunshine to
the day and remind us that no matter what situation
we find ourselves in, G-d is watching out for us."
**Chumi Friedman, Editor of Olam Yehudi
a publication of The Jewish Press**

"Everyday life can teach us uncommon wisdom.
Kugel Chaos & Unconditional Love is a delightful
collection of everyday stories which contain
uncommon gems of insight about our most
important relationships: friendship, love, marriage
and parenting. A very enjoyable and
growthful read!"
**Chaplain (COL-ret) Nosson Sachs,
Past Director of the US Army Strong Bonds
Relationship Enrichment Program**

"What a warm, friendly, upbeat read. I feel like I'm
sitting on your living room couch with you,
watching and observing your fun family

and your equally fun, vibrant, positive and
productive outlook on life".
Chana Weisberg, Editor
TheJewishWoman.org / Chabad.org

"Chana Gittle Deray's writing is a powerful antidote to
today's epidemic of cynicism and warped values.
With gentle humor and brilliant simplicity,
she sets us on the right path and we love her for it."
Rishe Deitsch, Senior Editor
N'shei Chabad Newsletter

"As parents we often need just one or two pieces of
the puzzle to make us feel like our lives can fit
together towards the future we envision; perspective,
humor, encouragement. Chana Gittle has placed
these for us in the pages of her book. We need only
pick it up and find a friend who has faith enough to
spare for us in our journey."
Deborah Gilboa, MD, Author,
Parenting and Youth Development Expert, AKA "Dr.G."

"It never fails! Every time I read Chana Gittle's writing,
it just lifts up my emotions, and usually puts a smile
on my face. Her innate wisdom, plus sweet sense of
humor really does what it's supposed to do... teach,
inspire, and, yes, entertain! It's truly intelligent
education combined with the power to make the
reader feel hopeful and at peace with the knowledge
that G-d is in charge!! Enjoy the book, gift the book
to friends and family."
Sarah Karmely, Internationally renowned Speaker,
Author, Counselor and Mentor

Kugel, Chaos & Unconditional Love

Chana Gittle Deray

Illustrations by Rivka B.Deray

ISBN: 1977769705
Library of Congress Cataloging-in-Publication Data
20179165048

SOUL
POTATO

New York, Jerusalem, Sydney, Chicago, Pittsburgh, Postville

**This book is available at a discount for
bulk purchases.
For more information visit our website at
chanagittlederay.com**

This Book is
Dedicated to...

Anyone who has taken on
the crazy-wonderful journey
to marry and raise a family,
the funniest, most unpredictable, meaningful and
important job and privilege you will ever have.

May you find the joy,
the laugh-out-loud moments,
the blessings and miracles
right in your own home.

~

Especially to my husband,
for his dedication to this wonderful adventure.
And to our children,
who make everything we do
worth doing.

In the merit of a refua shelema,
health, strength, and abundant nachas
For my parents
Yacov Yitzchok ben Osna &
Simma Nuta bas Rivka
&
Eternal Nachas to
My husband's parents
Raphoel ben Saul &
Bendkia bas Yosef

We are building upon the
greatness that you have built

Contents

My Carpet Tells a Story

A long with preparing for Passover, we were giving the house that extra shine as we got ready to welcome our guests. You know how it goes ... all of a sudden you see all the dust, dirt and repairs that are needed. After pricing floor refinishing for under the living room carpet, and learning we would need to move out for four days (who would want us?!) we called the carpet cleaners.

The two men showed up and got to work. "How old is this carpet? Are you sure it is only five years old? Boy, it's seen a lot of traffic, huh? What? Nine kids?", as they give you that look.

"Really! I've got two and that's plenty! Really, nine kids? Hey, this lady here's got nine kids!"

Both of them are looking at me now. *The look.* It's the same look the exterminator gave me years ago as he commented about all the then-young children busily crafting, eating, cutting and dancing all over the kitchen. "Whew!" he said to me, "What time do they all go home?" He looked bewildered upon learning that they *were* home and all belonged to me.

The carpet cleaners made numerous trips out to the truck for more chemicals, going over the darkened areas again and again, muttering as they worked: "...Can't imagine having nine of them. So I guess you all sit around over here a lot. And that path. They must have a *lot* of friends. They must play over here on the floor a lot. What happened over there? Sticky. Oh, a menorah tipped. Thought you guys kept them in the window...."

Scrubbing and spraying and rubbing and brushing, and shaking their heads in disbelief. Soon the two of them looked about as worn out as the carpet.

"Well ma'am, that's the best we can do. This carpet has sure seen a lot of wear and tear. You may want to consider refinishing the wood floor underneath. That would last you *foreva!*" So much for *"foreva."*, as they followed my glance to the worn out finish on my dining room floor.

The carpet cleaners left in both a chemical and cultural daze. I had to laugh – after all their work, the room really didn't look much different except that all of my furniture was now in the dining room with very clear markings of where it all would need to be put back. What had changed was the way I was looking at it all. They had uncovered some *Emes,* real truth. There it was, carved right into the carpet... proof of all our blessings – our family. There were the fun times, the holidays celebrated, the guests hosted, the little toy cars and trucks driven around, the many dances danced. It was a very fulfilled carpet. *Baruch Hashem*, thank G-d!

If we ever do refinish the floor underneath, we will need to bury the pieces of our carpet in that special place where they bury holy items that are no longer used.

Hey... Does anyone want house guests for four days?

Why Oh Why Oh Why?

I looked up from my work to find him down on one knee, with his shoulders squared and a quirky smile on his face.

"Will you marry me?"

He was kind, generous, smart and fun. He possessed an appreciation for life, and apparently, the other half of my soul. Besides, he knew how to cook. He was French, and while his accent was exciting to my friends, I wanted to understand him the first time he said something: "I'm sorry, did you say 'can' or 'can't' that time?" But in this instance, his words and intention were very clear.

He waited patiently for my answer. I searched my heart and gave him the only answer I could.

"Why?"

There was so much that most people based their lives on that I could not figure out. For instance: Who were "they", and why did what "they" were thinking, wearing or doing dictate what I was supposed to do? Why did some people consider themselves more valuable or important when we are all made of the same stuff? And why was embarrassing someone considered so powerful? Why was a secluded business dinner not considered a date? And why *did* people get married?

Still kneeling and apparently undaunted by my blank stare, he began to sing me a song. He must have sensed that although I was enjoying his performance that I really did need to know why. He began to share his dream of what he saw marriage being: Our relationship would be a priority, exclusive, and protected, a real partnership with a true connection, different than any other relationship – closer than a best friend or even family. A soul mate.

The kind man with the incomplete soul presented a worthy picture.

I said yes.

And then I panicked.

I had no idea how to create such a marriage, and I would accept nothing less. If I was going to do this, it would have to be worth doing.

As a graphic designer, I had mentors – people who had succeeded brilliantly in their craft. I traveled to hear them speak, sitting in the front row so that I could soak up all they had to offer. I would seek their guidance and gentle critique. Although I had seen many marriages, no one I knew lived the picture of marriage that he painted, and that I now wanted to build.

Although…

I saw sparks of it in his family. They were seven brothers and a dad. With their mother having passed away before we met, I could not learn from her, but I could see the legacy of what that marriage had created. Despite the prohibitive phone charges and poor connections at the time, I watched brothers call each other across continents, laughing and supporting one another, all at volumes that made me question the need for a phone at all. They would do any-thing for each other. This was what I wanted to build. Although maybe a quieter version.

I decided that whatever was done in my hus-band's home to yield such strength, we would do in ours. So when he said "I want to keep ko-sher and Shabbat" – traditions many European Jews keep – I replied, "Show me what to do."

I remembered Nana's kosher kitchen, with the layers of yellowed plastic lace-like table-cloths, and margarine instead of butter on the table. I loved margarine. This could work.

As for Shabbat? – I had carpooled to Hebrew school with a family who parked a camper behind the Jewish center for holidays. This was looking yummy, and adventurous.

My husband taught me what he knew, like taping light switches so that I wouldn't turn them on or off during Shabbos, how to soak and salt meat – not knowing that in America kosher meat was sold already soaked and salted – and other interesting things. Tootsie Rolls were out, and haircuts and yard sales would be replaced by leisurely meals, long walks, and time together. Saturday was now Shabbat – a day of rest.

Wanting to learn more, I sought out the wisdom of a kind, older rabbi in our town who had impressed me with the simplicity of his Yom Kippur sermon. After confirming that my husband would really be OK with this, he gave me a pile of books to read.

When he retired we found a congregation that was just forming, with a young rabbi and his wife. Although they were obviously over the top with their observance, there was a simple truth and a joyful warmth about them, and we became good friends. Together with other newcomers, we learned and did, each *mitzvah*, each commandment, opening up understanding for us to want the next. We were called *baal teshuvas*, or "BTs", meaning those who return to their faith. How could we return to a place we never stood before or even knew existed? We each have a soul that is connected to our Creator, the process of learning and doing mitzvoth, commandments, cleans up that connection so we can feel the closeness that is always there. The "return" is to our essence.

Wanting to add healthy and natural to our new dance, we left our BT cocoon and moved to Vermont. Without a true Torah presence in the area, we connected back to our over-the-top rabbi and his wife, who connected us to a few other over-the-top rabbis and their wives, and together we started creating that presence by running events. We would find the venue and send out the PR, while the children colored posters, and the rabbis added the soul. Our first matzah bakery – with hands-on demonstrations of the process of baking matzos, along with general education about the holiday of Passover – was an overwhelming success. It attracted much curiosity: Local Jewish people who knew little or nothing of their roots came, school superintendents, public officials and some who were excited to try the delicacies a bakery named "Matzah" would certainly produce.

One of our matzah-bakery rabbis soon started driving an hour each way to our home to teach us Torah – a living breathing instruction manual from our Creator to tell us how to use all we had been designed with to its greatest potential. And there was instruction on just about every-thing: business, food, science, morality, personal growth and relationships. These guys discussed "Mars and Venus" before anyone had even thought of how the differences between men and women relate to our interpersonal relation-ships. And there are scientific facts that are just now being discovered. Torah is a parenting guide par excellence and a marriage guide with laws that when followed have the power to build a marriage strong and complete. Although marriage is not easy, starting your life based on the premise that a husband and wife are two halves of one soul changes everything that comes afterwards.

At first, I questioned everything, needing the whys and how-comes for every new mitzvah. After time, it became like turning the key to my car: No need to know about the pistons and electronics; I trusted it would get me there and I just wanted to go!

Learning how powerful our Hebrew names were, we started using them, and began cele-brating our birthdays on the Hebrew calendar. My husband wanted to wear a kippah, and I felt drawn to cover my hair – "Just do it." was a friend's response. And I did.

And it was there, on that mountain in Vermont – where most people just become alcoholics, and perhaps some would have preferred that we did – that things flipped: instead of "*living* life, and *doing* mitzvot" we were now "*living* mitzvot, and *doing* life." And the more we did, the more life came into focus. Sort of....

As someone who did not grow up with these traditions – or even have a point of reference with which to approach some of them – my enthusiasm and lack of information made for a powerful *and* klutzy existence:

I had been learning about the laws governing male/female interactions: Because marriage holds the potential for the holiest thing we can do on this earth – to bring a soul down into this world, there are laws to protect marriage, to keep it pure, fresh and long lasting. One afternoon, I was out driving alone and noticed our rabbi standing on the road beside his minivan a few miles from his home. I pulled over to see if he was OK. He asked if I would take him home and I proudly told him "No." I drove off wondering why he was not more careful with something as important as a woman not being alone with a man who was not her husband, and I started looking for a "kosher" solution. I drove to the rabbi's house, and asked his wife to loan me a few of their children, which of course she wanted to know what for. I proudly explained that it was in order to drive the rabbi home in a proper manner, and that I had left him on the side of the road with a broken down car. In her gracious and delicate manner she explained: "Chana Gittle, there are nuances that we need to learn." As she explained these to me, in walked the rabbi, head lowered and shaking it side to side.

A Baal Teshuva is a terrible thing to waste.

And then there was the Rosh Hashanah I had learned about the tradition of putting symbolic foods on the table, to bring blessings for the new year: With my family all dressed up and seated around the beautifully set table, I began my parade of symbolic foods: First the apples and honey, for a sweet new year. Next the pomegranate, that our merits should be abundant. I continued my procession as the little faces resting close to the table examined each delicacy with excitement. Finally, I put out the large fish head, symbolizing our desire to lead with our head – with a vision, rather than be a follower, or tail. Feeling like quite the balabusta, I proudly took my seat next to my husband. The room was quiet as the children stared at the fish head with varying degrees of shock and disgust. My husband leaned over towards me and gently whispered: "... Do you think that maybe you should have cooked it first?"

The details would come with time. Until then I imagined that Hashem, G-d, was very happy, and thoroughly entertained.

It seemed that I needed to ask more questions. In fact, each time I felt lost or frustrated, confused or confined, I learned that I was just not asking enough questions. In Judaism, questions are very encouraged. Which was good, because we had so many of them. Afraid of overwhelming our kind rabbi, I assembled a corps of rabbis: some far away for more personal questions; others for specific questions; one who was exceedingly gentle; and another who we were told would crawl through a vault of books until he found our answer. I then added one more – to spread the wealth, leaving no rabbi with a unduly heavy burden – or to realize how little I knew.

As we journeyed to bigger cities to find yeshivahs for the children, who were now growing in years and number, we realized that learning Torah on a mountain top through stories of sages – with our squadron of rabbis and their families as our only role models – had left us painfully idealistic. Jewish people are human and fail sometimes – even the observant ones. We all have something to work on and while I might be able to hide my stuff neatly inside, others have more exposed challenges. And then there were those who we only hoped to become like: a woman who stands in all weather collecting money for people she doesn't know; a rabbi who stood up to his biggest supporter, willing to give up his dream, in order to protect the education of one child; a woman who stands each day in front of a supermarket encouraging people to do a deed of kindness; a young couple who fills their Shabbat table each week beyond reasonable capacity with total strangers.

Why?

Because they are not strangers. Each of us has a piece of G-d in us, which makes us all family. Funky at times, but still family. And our Father, no matter what we do or don't do, we are all His beloved and worthy children. There is nothing we can do to harm the love He has for us. Ever. And the Torah is His gift, our birthright, our instruction manual.

I had no idea that this is what being a Jew was. It was as if I had been using this instructional manual called Torah to prop open a window while I ran the program called life at a fraction of its potential. Well, no longer.

What began as a quest for a recipe for marriage became a door into a world I am grateful to be "returning" to. Although wearing stockings to the beach, and Passover cleaning both terrified me, the payoff has always been more than what I put in. Other than the fish head, the laws and traditions never asked anything of us that was not pleasant or good. In them, we found that each person is invaluable; and to embarrass someone is equivalent to killing him; and that yes, a secluded dinner *is* a date. And I've even learned that a fish head can be quite tasty to some when cooked first.

There is a deep respect for life, for people, and especially for women. Each time I learn more, I am grateful for the *emes*, the pure truth of what I knew deep inside, all from a source written at the beginning of time that is eternal, defined and consistent.

I have found a new rhythm for life – a lively Chassidic beat called *chayus* – a pounding inside when you are in sync with who you are and where you should be. It's the high on the mountain that you wish you could bottle while you figure out how to generate more tomorrow. It's the power of love and giving and joy that bubbles up and over-the-top causing you to sound really odd, with a smile that looks like you slept with a matzah stretching the corners of your mouth.

Although some may shudder at our over-the-top lifestyle, I shudder at the thought of not having it. The original plan was to be bold and have three children. We had no idea how bold bold could be, or how miraculous it would be to raise each one of them. It is through these children that I have those mentors and role models for the type of person I am working to become. Any thoughts of a shiny new coupe at this stage have been replaced with carpooling in a 15 passenger van not even from this decade, with a view of the street underneath and sometimes a square of American cheese stuck to the window. Much cooler. But definitely not a quieter version of my husband's family.

With all I have learned, I still can't always tell if the Frenchman/Chassid is saying 'can' or 'can't', but I will be forever grateful that he stayed on one knee and stopped singing long enough to answer my question… "Why?"

A Rat's Tale

A number of years ago, my husband and I rented a beautiful home in Squirrel Hill, Pennsylvania. It was one of those spacious, oversized brick homes with large windows and warm wonderful woodwork throughout. It had more bedrooms and bathrooms than we had ever had. It also had a great big kitchen. This is a real treat in Pittsburgh, where closet-sized kitchens are the norm. And wonderful large closets. Even more of a treat here, where having closets is not the norm, unless you are referring to the size of the kitchens. Absolutely a dream home! Oh, and did I mention, it had its own rats' nest under the porch.

Now, had either my husband or I been a research scientist, this would have been a terrific opportunity. However, with many lively children running around, it was... crazy! With Derays having notoriously large feet, it was not hard to figure out whose footprints were tracking through the place. There was a rat amongst us!

At the hardware supercenter, Mr. Deray found a new type of trap. It stuck to the floor and the rodent would theoretically step on it and get stuck to the adhesive surface. Unfortunately, we seemed to have super-strength rats who stepped on the traps and walked off with them stuck to their feet. We now had rats in tap shoes. We had no choice but to call in an exterminator.

"Hmmmm...", he hmmm-ed, as he shook his head from side to side with a very dark and serious expression, "This *isn't good*."

So began the nightly visits from the exterminator. "Maman, the Rat Man is here."

"Honey, please don't call him that. He has a name!"

The exterminator would show up each evening to lay out the traps. The first few nights he used apples as bait. The next few times he used peanut butter. One night he showed up with his wife's chicken. I could not resist the challenge. I suggested setting half the traps with her recipe, and the remainder with my own house recipe, and we would see whose chicken was truly to die for. All in all, he caught about 45 rats. The results of the taste-off will forever remain a secret.

The rats became part of our lively household. Although this could have been quite a dangerous situation, they came out mostly late at night and when the house was quiet. Sometimes we would spy an unwanted visitor attempting to join our Shabbat celebration and would tap our feet in a wild dance under the table, sending him back to his hideout, while our guests looked on with curiosity. If I had to go downstairs in the middle of the night I would proceed with heavy footsteps, yelling in my huskiest Mafioso voice, "*You dirty rats... I'm coming down!*"

One morning, I joined my husband at the dining room table, where he was enjoying a peaceful breakfast. As I sat there, I heard a scurrying sound coming from inside the oversized garbage can just a few feet away. I quietly whispered to my husband, "I think there is a rat in the garbage can."

He continued with his breakfast, calmly answering, "I know."

Hmm. I quietly mentioned, "Maybe we should do something about it."

"I put it in there."

He put it in there? How could he!? What was he thinking? Although the corners of my mouth revealed my true horror, I spoke in my most pleasant voice. "Why did you do that?"

I had his full attention now. He answered with deep sincerity, "What else should I have done with it?"

So, he's comfortable with this idea. I thought I knew him. Could this be the same man who elegantly eats watermelon with a fork and knife? The man who is so careful with issues of germs and cleanliness? The rats must be getting to him. Stay calm, Chana Gittle, remember... *sholom bayis,* peace in the home is most important.

We sat there together, him casually having breakfast, me wondering who he really was, and how he could be sitting there so calmly with a rat running around in the garbage can only a few feet away. He attempted to soothe my squeamishness. "It's fine. Don't worry about it." He smiled.

"Breakfast?"

All of a sudden, the rat was out of the can, literally, and running across the dining room floor. It must have kicked up enough momentum to knock the garbage can over. As it fled across the floor, my stunned husband sat bolt upright, looked at me and said, "There was a rat in the garbage can!"

"Really!?"

As it turns out, my husband had gotten up earlier and found himself in the company of a rat. A *different* rat! With great chivalry and some help from a broom, he had heroically protected his family, placing the rat's remains very thoughtfully in the *outside* garbage can. We had rat A, rat B; indoor can, outdoor can. Of course!

I felt like such a rat.

I must confess getting caught doing this dance on other occasions. You know, that crazy three step with husband wife and the *Yetzer Horah,* our evil inclination, all waltzing chaotically around, brilliantly choreographed to chase the G-dly presence out of the house. Well, *Baruch Hashem*, not today!

In the end, the rats proved more determined to live in the house than we were. We packed up our lively children, and possibly award winning chicken, and moved to a charming home with warm wonderful woodwork. It had cozy bedrooms and bathrooms, a dainty Pittsburgh kitchen, darling cubbyholes that would be flattered to be called closets, and no nightly visitors. Of the trapping sort anyway.

The Gift of a Soul

I t was a regular trip to the supermarket until I rounded the corner of the dairy aisle a little too enthusiastically, almost bumping into a well-dressed pretty dark haired woman. As I went to apologize, I noticed she had been crying.

"Is everything OK?

It's not fair to ask a woman who's holding it together with all that she has if she's OK, but my words were out before I could stop myself. She looked into my eyes, struggling to respond as the dam gave way, releasing the inexhaustible amount of tears that a woman's heart can hold.

Dancing between crying and apologizing she finally calmed herself and spoke:

"I had a miscarriage."

We held each other's hands doing that crazy thing women do – sharing something deeply intimate with a woman she just met in the cottage cheese aisle of the supermarket.

"It's so silly, really" she continued, "It was over a year ago... but some days... I don't know why... it's still so hard for me."

I wanted to comfort her, to give her hope and let her know that this is how it starts sometimes. And that it wasn't silly at all. I wanted her to know that I understood.

I understood the pain in her eyes; she needed to ask questions that had no answers. She needed someone to hear how she had it all there... and then it was not. She needed validation for all that she put into this – the love, the anticipation, the dreams – and to know that somewhere in the world, *something* had changed as a result of her uniquely creative feminine energy. She needed to express the hurt and shame she felt from the clumsily loving words offered by others, "next time don't..." and "just move on", as if it were somehow her fault and that it all meant nothing. She needed to know that she didn't do a thing in the world wrong – that it was all part of a plan that was bigger than she was. She needed to hear the story of the prince.*

~ ~ ~

Hundreds of years ago, there lived a very special rabbi, Rabbi Israel Baal Shem Tov, who was known throughout Europe as someone willing to do anything, even perform a miracle, in order to help another person.

One evening a middle-aged couple came to him. They desperately wanted a child. The Baal Shem Tov closed his eyes, allowing his consciousness to soar to the spiritual realms. Looking up at them sadly he said: "There is nothing I can do. Continue your prayers and good deeds and may Hashem, G-d, have mercy."

The wife burst into tears; "No, I won't accept that answer! I know that when a righteous person such as you decrees, Hashem must fulfill. I want a child!"

Her cry broke the rabbi's heart. He again lowered his head, this time for a long time, he then again looked up at the couple, "Next year you will have a child."

And so it was. The next year the woman gave birth to a beautiful baby boy. The couple's joy knew no bounds. The child was beautiful, with a sparkle in his eyes, and they could see that he was special – walking and talking at a very early age, and hungry for knowledge. They made plans to visit the holy Rabbi on the child's second birthday to show him what his blessing had produced, but on the morning of his second birthday the child did not wake up.

The parents mourned the traditional one week, and then set off to see the Baal Shem Tov. With swollen tear filled eyes they cried; "It was hard enough all those years to have no children, but to have loved and nurtured a child only to lose him… we can't understand."

The Baal Shem Tov understood better than they could possibly have imagined. "I have a story to tell you", he said:

A long time ago, there lived a rich and powerful king who longed for a son to carry on his lineage. He ordered that all his subjects hold daily prayers in their houses of worship so that G-d would grant him an heir.

One of his advisors, known for his hatred towards Jews, told the king that the reason he was still child-less was that his Jewish subjects were not praying for him sincerely enough, and the only way to make them do so was to oppress them. So the king issued a proclamation: If the queen is not blessed with a child within the next three months, all the Jews would be expelled from his kingdom."

A call resounded through the heavens for a soul willing to descend into the spiritually desolate environment of the royal palace in order the save the Jews of that land. One very holy soul agreed to make the sacrifice.

Very soon, the queen became pregnant and gave birth to a son. By the age of 2, the child could already read and write, and when he was 5 years old he had surpassed all his teachers. The king brought in many scholars, who filled the boy with wisdom and right-eous ideas. Influenced by this learning, the boy soon

left the palace and became a great and famous sage,
living a life of saintliness and good deeds.

When this sage passed on from this world and his
soul went up to the heavens, there wasn't a place holy enough for his special soul. The only problem was
it had one blemish – the fact that it had been conceived, born, and nurtured for two years in the spiritual void of the royal palace.

The Baal Shem Tov looked at the broken parents,
"In order for that soul to achieve its full potential, it
needed to return to earth to be conceived, given birth
to and nurtured in an atmosphere of holiness and
goodness."

"I saw that you were not destined to have children. But I also saw the depths of your pure desire
for a child, and knew you were the parents for this
special mission.

"That soul needed you to complete its mission in
the world."

~ ~ ~

While I struggled to get through the last
words of the story, we wiped our tears with
every sleeve and hem we could find. I pity the
poor soul who only needed some butter and had
no warning of what he was in for in the dairy
aisle.

I was told this story by a kind rabbi when I
stood in those same broken shoes.

At the beginning of our baby boom, we be-
friended a couple in our apartment building
who shared a similar due date and obstetrician,

but a different fate: Their pregnancy would pro-
gress, while ours would end early on.

Weeks later, my neighbor found herself with
no partner for her weekly Lamaze class and
asked if I would go with her. We were an odd
couple, but why not?

After a few rounds of focused breathing, the
women headed to the break room like a stam-
pede of blessed pachyderms. Once seated, they
began a kvetch session par excellence: restless
sleep, awkward bodies, cramping legs, yearn-
ings for beer and other parts of their lives back.
I stood aching, listening from behind a door –
how I longed to be where these women stood,
my body able to do what theirs was doing,
wondering if it ever would, and if I could offer
up a prayer of gratitude on my first varicose
vein if I was fortunate enough to acquire one in
this way.

Would I have recognized the absolute miracle
of a baby, or the trust that had been given to us
to raise it? Or would I have just thought of it as
a given, like going from the fourth grade to the
fifth – you get married and a child comes, right?
Not always. Sometimes you need to storm the
heavens, pleading for a soul to be sent down –
but oh, how special those souls are. This beautiful woman needed to know that pregnancy
would never be the same again – it would be

soooooo much scarier, and never taken for granted.

She needed to know that instead of attending a "Mommy and Me" class, where women gather to complain about unexciting existences, she should opt for time at the lobster tank at Walmart, G-d please forgive me, and swap phone numbers with moms who beam with enchantment and have crazy senses of humor. And when friends talked of "terrible twos" and "have you considered that someday they'll be teenagers," she will smile, knowing that she's been waiting for all those stages when souls reveal their passions and energy.

And none of it will be easy.

She will use strengths and talents she never had before, and wonder how she will fill her days with something as hair-raising and fulfilling once her children are grown. You see, although her pregnancy did not create a child, this not-child had created a mother – one who will forever live her life through a lens of gratitude.

As the containers of milk and cottage cheese came back into focus, we laughed as we pulled ourselves back together. We exchanged names, hugs and blessings, parting with a special closeness and added strength from each other.

I have not seen this woman since that day. She is a prominent business woman in our city, and I blow her a kiss each time I pass her place of business. I pray that the depths of her cries and pure desire for a child broke through the heavens. I know that she will pass that story on to the next woman who needs it, probably while standing in the supermarket or other such intimate place, sobbing together as she shares the words: "That soul needed *you.*"

* Excerpted from *The Reincarnated Prince* on Chabad.org

Splitting the Sea: Activating the Positive

W e might have a hole in our roof.

That's okay... it will be in good company with the hole behind the couch. It's not that we don't care about our home. In fact, that's how we *got* the hole behind the couch in the first place. We were having a broken pipe replaced. On his way out, the plumber sheepishly mentioned, "...Ma'am, you may want to call a drywall guy to look at the hole in your wall.

"But we don't have a hole...." Well, at least we didn't until he arrived. At that moment I knew with perfect faith that *Moshiach*, the messiah, would be here before the drywall guy, and we might never again be able to move that little couch in front of the hole.

In the late 1900's BCE (Before Children Existed), I could not understand how children with mismatched gloves were out in public places, and how much time and effort it really *can* take to change a light bulb, hang a fixture, or spackle a wall. Even once children did exist, we ran our home with the precision of a well-oiled submarine crew, with schedules and command posts for each ensign. Ours would have been the submarine rocking side to side, but it would have been orderly.

As life flourished, I found myself promoted to head of triage, dancing as fast as I could to keep up with the incoming wounded and special requests. At this stage, a dent in a wall or a roof that doesn't actively leak gets elevated to the level of a mitzvah: it is a mitzvah to leave an area of the home unfinished to represent the destruction of the great Temple in Jerusalem. Our home does not forget the destruction, it weeps alongside it. Gratefully, life is full, and it seems frivolous to get overexcited about a roof that leaked only once. Besides... I only seem to remember it on Shabbat – that's when it seems to rain, and that's when I remember things that I can't do anything about, since on Shabbat no work is done.

I can't even remember the circumstances that caused the roof to leak. It had never leaked before, and hasn't leaked since. Not even the time I heard we were getting one of those great Pittsburgh downpours and came running home, as if standing there looking up at the ceiling would actually help in some way. I put a bucket in the hallway – providing the children a chance to put their foot into it – and started researching roofers. When the storm ended, the bucket remained empty of both drips and feet. I thanked Hashem and got back to our crazy wonderful dance, forgetting the roof once again. One time it rained for days – no leak. Even with a hurricane, no leak! Truthfully, though, even a one-time leak could have caused damage along the walls, ceiling, and furniture, right down to the foundation. Water could have gotten in, weakening the stones and mortar, allowing mold, mildew, and other undesirable things to grow, heaven forbid.

I was thinking about the roof the other day. It was Shabbat and I should have been thinking more worthy thoughts, but my heart was aching over news of a different type of destruction – that of a wonderful family. They lived in a faraway state so I would not be seeing them that Shabbat, but as much as I tried, my mind kept wandering back to the family and the roof. There seemed to be a connection.

Somehow, in that family, there was a vulnerability. Perhaps even a small hole that no one was aware of, a weakness just large enough for something unwanted to slowly seep in, allowing something undesirable to grow. In time, the foundation was ruined, the walls and furnishings destroyed. Lives changed forever. This family would now be living under two separate roofs.

Don't all of our relationships have those vulnerable spots? Sometimes they form over time, from wear and tear or difficult circumstances. In one small moment the roof can give out, allowing an unkind thought, word or action to seep in. If only the repair was as easy as calling a roofer. But G-d would never leave us without instructions.

The Talmud states: "Making a match between two people is as difficult as the Splitting of the Red Sea." *Oy*. These may be comforting words when the going is a bit rough, but as far as ad campaigns go, it is not very inspiring. Can you imagine if the army advertised this way? Instead of, "Join the army, see the world," or, "Be all that you can be!" try, "Join the army and fill your body with shrapnel."

I'm not inspired.

But what if we hear these words not as a warning, or even as words of comfort, but as an instruction. ...*Go split the sea!* Hang in there with me. This actually works.

Have you ever heard someone say, "I'm drowning!"... in laundry, paperwork, to-do lists, emails, challenges, even worthy resolutions. I recently heard a speaker say that if we don't wake up with ADD, then we are certainly there by the time we go to sleep. There is technology we can't figure out, and technology we have figured out that is now figuring us out. There's too much information. We can't even make a simple dinner anymore. We need to chop the right vegetables in the proper color spectrum sautéed in the correct oils. Have you tried to buy shampoo or bandages? Why are there so many types and so many places to buy them? There's an ever growing sense that nothing is good enough.

We live in a time of great abundance! I have a friend who often reminds me that the many tuition bills to pay, shoes to buy, and clothing to mend are truly all signs of great blessing. It's all good! But even wonderful can be overwhelming. I love dessert. I adore curling up on our little couch with a book. Jewish music can feel like oxygen to me. However, I would not be soothed by being forced fed cheesecakes while duct taped to the couch as my favorite song played loud enough to melt the speakers. It's all good...

but maybe just a little more than any of our
senses can handle.

So how do we split the sea?

It's almost the end of another normal busy
day. Your mind is in two places and your body
in a third. You find the happy helpful crew in
the bathroom. The three little boys are helping
you by "washing" the baby. Your toddler smiles
at you proudly as he scrubs the commode with
your husband's toothbrush. And the twins who
have been bathed and dressed are now back in
the bathtub, still bathed and dressed, and are
playing happily in the water you forgot to drain.
You could laugh, but your mind is going over
the list of things you need to accomplish once
they are all tucked into bed, which now seems
like a faraway dream. Your husband walks
through the door.

What if you drop everything and "split the
sea." Dive into his presence – greet him with
your full attention as if you are "walking
through on dry land": a place free of all that you
were drowning in the moment before he arrived. You know what dry land is: It's that place
your mind goes when you decide you are on vacation and nothing else matters. As a kid it was
a snow day.

What if in the middle of the week you "split
the sea" by putting everything and everyone on
hold and go for a walk or a cup of coffee togeth-

er. Pretend you are on vacation. Only talk of positive matters, and don't try to solve *anything*. Spend a moment simply to reconnect, giving uninterrupted attention – a moment of intimacy. Perhaps you could even go away for a few days. The fantastic thing about doing this is that it all just stays there, just as the walls of the Red Sea did, and it will all come crashing right back down when you return. But a few days on dry land can be *amazingly* refreshing for a relationship. By connecting with each other, you bring G-d into the relationship. Where there is peace between husband and wife, that's where you will find Hashem. When the waters return, now it's truly the three of you, and there is *nothing* you cannot handle together.

What if we split the sea for our children and really tune in: Taste his feelings of success as he memorizes his speech, join her as she shows you the video she made, listen as another child describes her dreams for her future and favorite memories from her past. Really look at each of them. Pause and say nothing. Listen to their minds, instead of your own.

What if we get off our email when our children call home (they hear us typing), and go to that spot. You know the one. That spot on the couch that you gravitate to when an old friend calls, where you sit on one knee and gaze out the window into nothingness, where time does not exist, dinner is happily burning, the kids are wearing your old shoes and strumming brooms and mops while the smoke alarm sings high harmony... and it's all beautiful, because you are sitting there, connecting with someone you love.

But what if they don't respond? What if no one wants to join you on dry land?

I once asked one of my boys why the good can be so hard to notice. Why is it so much easier to complain than to appreciate? Why, in a day where seven things go right, does the one thing that went wrong block out all the good, the way holding a thumb up to an eye blocks out an entire room? He explained to me that negativity is the default mode in the world we live in right now. Positivity is actually stronger, but needs effort in order to be used. It needs to be activated.

"Splitting the sea" is a recipe for intimacy – something humans cannot live without. Intimacy is the glue of our relationships, the protection against the elements, the glue for our roofs, our lives and the lives of our families. The potential is there, we only need to activate it with our efforts – our thoughts, speech, and actions.

So what are we waiting for?

There are only a few moments remaining to activate the positive before Moshiach and the drywall guy arrive. With our new recipe and Hashem's help, none of us will *ever* have to think about a hole in a roof again.

The Irreplaceable Woman of Valor

I t was one of those moments that should be bronzed.

My husband was on the phone, attempting to increase the face value of my life insurance policy. He was a seasoned insurance agent, and knew exactly how much was needed. The representative was insisting that the amount was extravagant for a woman who *just* stayed at home, living a low-risk existence. Clearly he had never seen me teach our children to drive, nor had he tasted some of the dinners that I cook.

He then implied some kind of sinister intent, as if he'd been a victim of too many mystery novels. That's when my husband said those precious words:

"Listen... Bill Gates could not afford to replace what my wife does for this family." I imagined being able to *hear* the representative's eyebrows rising on the other end of the phone line. In the end, my husband triumphed! And so did my self-esteem.

I lived for a long time on those words.

It didn't bother me in the least when a guest, upon observing our lively living room full of young children all very close in age commented, "Do you know that this would be illegal if they weren't all yours?"

Or when the cashier who rang up my back to school order discovered that I was not a teacher, but a mother of many, and announced to anyone within earshot, *"Wow...!* I thought only people in third world countries had that many children!"

Nope. Nothing could bother me.

But I've always wondered, if I calculated the numbers, what a woman who *just stays at home* was worth. Or as King David says in the Book of Psalms, "Who can replace her?"

Let's find out!

We'll start with food. I'll call my old neighbor – she's a caterer. Between the two of us we have over 20 children and the year that we lived across the street from one another was infused with laughter. We once ended up sitting next to each other at a benefit concert. The organizers had flown a singer in from Israel who had the most magnificent voice I have ever heard – pure, clear, full of life. She hit notes that could have shattered the curtains. Tired from a busy day, we slid into our theater seats as if we were sliding into home base. As the lights went down I whispered, "I have an icepack. Want to share?"

She whispered back, "I once asked my daughter to bring me something cold for my back, and she brought me a frozen chicken!"

We were gone! The fatigue and stress of the day, the pure beautiful high pitched singing, the camaraderie of a friend who knows how to laugh... it was like a diamond cutter hitting the stone at just the right angle. I stuffed my scarf into my mouth to muffle my cries of laughter. Then, through our tears, we noticed the organizers of the event sitting in the seats in front of us. The perfect storm.

"Hey, Miriam, it's Chana Gittle. Tell me what it would cost for you to provide three freshly cooked meals a day, for my entire family plus guests, for a year." She's laughing. "Just pretend I'm Bill Gates." Now she's really laughing. "Can you get back to me with those numbers?"

We will also need a counselor. I can just see making *that* call:

"Yes, I'm looking to hire an experienced counselor for a large group of children. Someone caring who will listen, advise them about life, troubleshoot their challenges, and be on call 24 hours a day."

"No problem, Mrs. Deray. Now you just hold on over there, hon…we're sending someone right over… Just stay calm… and away from any frozen chickens."

I better Google that one. Yearly salary for a counselor: $60,000

Next, a year's worth of laundry for our size family. If I call, they're going to hang up on me. *I would hang up on me!* I had better Google that one too. In fact we can just Google the rest. Laundry: $18,000.

Transportation: We'll need someone who can strategically bang the gas tank on the old 15 passenger van to start her, then keep her calm while kids laugh, sing and shriek, and drive stealthily enough for them to do their homework. Chauffeur: $22,000

We'll need an activities director: $37,000; and an advocate to hover in the emergency room and doctor's office, to remind everyone to wash their hands and to ask too many questions. My dentist once fielded my child's inquiry back to me: "Ask your Mom what that's for, she must have the equivalent of a two-year dental degree by now."

We will also need a handyman for reattach-
ing knobs, light painting and plumbing...
someone who really gets the power of duct tape:
$35,000. How about a bloodhound for finding
lost objects: $1000; and one of those big guys
with a hard hat and reflector vest to stand with
his arms folded and oversee that homework and
jobs are completed on time, according to specifi-
cations, and that no one is writing their names
in the dust: $58,000.

A carpenter. When I am pregnant I build furniture. Possibly a reaction to the extra iron in the
prenatal vitamins: $40,000

For conflict management, someone with the
wisdom of Solomon, a real negotiator, to decide:
whose turn it is, whose job it is and what to
serve for supper when everyone likes something
else. I wonder what Henry Kissinger is up to
these days. $515,000.

Oooh... how about an air traffic controller, to
keep track of everyone's trajectories. A bit
pricey, but worth every penny: $108,000. We
better order some snacks. I've heard that they
sometimes go on strike if they are not happy.

Perhaps one of those guys from NASA who
figures out the window of opportunity for
launching the shuttle, to help decide when everyone can get together for a celebration, a vacation, a family photo, or to start Passover cleaning: $78,000.

A few years ago when I went for job place-
ment testing, the counselor read my results with
a curious look. "I know that your background is
in art, but your job profile keeps coming up *military.*"

We will also need an organizer; a custodial
service; a tutor; a party planner for birthdays,
bar mitzvahs and weddings; a kosher kitchen
supervisor; an actuary to get the true picture of
the risks involved when signing field trip waiv-
ers, and a chaperone for said field trips – someone who can ice skate and is not afraid to get on
a horse or put their hand in the piranha tank.

Are you sitting a little taller yet? This is better
for the posture than a Pilates class!

How about an archeologist to sort out the
freezer before Passover, and to identify what is
distilling in backpacks left in the closet through
winter break; a fashion designer – to ensure that
the family doesn't look like a clown parade on
family outings; a mechanical engineer to figure
out how to put together toys; a rocket scientist
to open the stroller; an epidemiologist to deter-
mine if play dates, sleepovers, and family visits
are safe.

We need someone who doesn't mind that any
closed door quickly becomes an information
booth: Tap, tap, tap, "Do you know where...
why... how much... and what time...?"

And if this is to be realistic, we'll also need someone to kill all the houseplants, and assure the neighbors that although they don't hear the smoke alarm every night at dinnertime anymore, the children *are* being fed. A concierge: $22,000

We better get some more snacks – we will need something yummy to feed the officials when they show up to see who all these people are spilling out onto the front lawn. And tell the caterer we'll get back to her with some new numbers. Better yet, for $22,000 we'll hire a cook.

I once had a neighbor who was a disaster management expert. That made two of us. And no one knows how to stretch time, money, and all her resources like a mother of many children.

Could a price be paid for someone who will take a pure leap of faith, bringing as many souls into the world as G-d will allow, putting her life and waistline on hold, taking care to do it all within the framework of the laws that Hashem has given her to keep?

Someone who will smile although her heart is crying, speak softly when her insides beg to SCREAM, who will dispense hope, optimism, and that special serenity and trust in Hashem when every cell of her being is terrified? Someone who will devote her life to building foundations. And perhaps the most important job of all

– to be happy, so fulfilled in her G-d given role that it overflows on to all that are around her. No stuntman alive would attempt such a feat.

So, Bill Gates… where are we holding?

I always dreamed of being somebody. And I truly am. We all are.

To our husbands, families…to G-d… and sometimes even to the insurance company, we are the irreplaceable and eternally invaluable, women of valor.

Of Menorahs, Ladders, and Crazy Lit-up Rabbis

I t was a typical Tuesday in suburbia – not an election day, not a recycling day, and not any other Tuesday of great significance.

Or so I thought.

I had driven over to Miriam's house, a warm and wonderful place to go for a cup of tea and some lively conversation. We were doing what we often did on a weekday, standing in her hallway chatting, with our children hard at play nearby, when in walked her husband, wearing a *kapoteh*, the traditional Chassidic frock coat worn on holidays and the Sabbath, and a very lit-up smile. He continued up the steps, greet-

ting us with a hearty, joy-filled, sing-song: *"Gut Yom Tov, gut Yom Tov!* – Happy Holiday!"

What could have gotten into this rabbi now?

This was the rabbi whose overly inspired voice I heard each evening as I picked up the phone during what my friend calls "happy hour" – children busy with all the creative and wondrous things they do before tiring out themselves and everything around them for the evening. He would ask with such joy filled enthusiasm, "Can your husband make the *minyan*, a quorum of ten men for prayer?" You would have thought he was inviting my husband to a party for a king.

As far as it being a holiday? I may not have been aware of all the details of living as an observant Jew back then, but I was pretty sure that if it were a holiday, I would have known about it. Miriam and I paused our conversation, returned the rabbi's curious greeting – Miriam looking a little apologetic – and watched in silence as the lit-up rabbi disappeared down the hallway. I couldn't help but think, "Man... he is *so* over the top! Of course it's *Yom Tov* on his planet today. In fact, I bet it's always *Yom Tov* on his planet. This rabbi should not be let out of the house unless under proper supervision."

And this was not the only rabbi we had met from the over-the-top rabbi department.

There was another wonderful, although slightly distracted, rabbi that we became close with at the time. With that same look of joy and selfless love in his eyes, this rabbi would build this fantastically oversized menorah, at a Shell gas station that looked out onto a major intersection where three towns met. It was truly awe-inspiring.

We would bring our children after dark on Chanukah to the gas station to watch. Up and down the ladder went the determined rabbi, with a blowtorch in hand, lighting large oil lanterns, in spite of rain, wind, or anything else G-d would send his way. We stood nearby – his wife and their children, us and our children, our necks craned, mouths open, noses running – the perfect rent-a-crowd. Up and down the ladder to the enormous menorah he went, hoping to reach out to any Jew who happened to drive by. What a sight. After finally getting the torches to stay lit, he would recite the prayers in a calm and splendidly beautiful voice. Then, while still on the ladder and holding his torch, he would prepare to sing. We stood by with great anticipation as he opened his mouth to sing the first line of "Maoz Tzur, Rock of Ages'" when instead he belted out in a hardy voice *"Haneirot Halalu."*

Now, any rabbi worth his weight in chocolate coins knows that *everyone* sings "Rock of Ages" after lighting the menorah! And if you are not going to sing "Rock of Ages," how about "Hatikvah," or a little "Havah Nagilah"? We looked up at him, singing with such heartfelt sincerity after all his hard work up and down the ladder, using his remaining strength on this odd little tune, and thought, "Where on the planet did the rabbi get this song from? If he wants to start drawing a *real* crowd out here, he's going to have to learn the traditional tunes."

After years of watching these and other animated, enthusiastic rabbis, with their interesting and industrious ways of approaching the holidays – and every day for that matter – I have learned that sometimes it's *me* who is missing a tune.

As it turns out, the odd little song the rabbi insisted on singing after lighting his majestic menorah, "Haneirot Halalu," is a beautifully powerful and traditional song that tells us why we light the candles, their meaning, and all about the miracle of the lights. I have learned to sing this song as heartily as any rabbi on a ladder, hitting its low, low notes and all, but more importantly, my family now sings it with great joyful chaos by the light of their own menorahs and lit-up smiles.

I have also learned that Miriam's husband actually *was* inviting my husband to a party for a king each night – our King, G-d, who rejoices in hearing from us three times a day, with extra pleasure when we call with a group of ten men.

And about that random Tuesday... it turns out that it was not so random after all. It was Yud-Tes Kislev, a day celebrating a string of miraculous events that allowed the spreading of Chassidus, the inner dimension of Torah, to the world. Who knew?

But now, I've got it. In fact, I've got it so bad that I also walk around on Yud-Tes Kislev wishing heartfelt "Gut Yom Tov!" and talking to complete strangers about bringing light into the world.

I feel grateful to Miriam's husband, the Shell gas station rabbi, and the many over-the-top rabbis who wear *kapotehs* on random Tuesdays and sing odd little songs while standing on ladders with torches while it rains – rabbis who welcome every Jew with warmth and an open heart, no matter how little we yet know or do, and despite how awfully know-it-all we can be. Thanks for putting yourselves out there – looking a little different at times, so that those of us who were not given our heritage at birth, can have another chance to receive what is our birthright. Our Torah.

A little knowledge can be a dangerous thing, but being a little "lit-up" can dispel a lot of darkness.

Maman's Latke Recipe

L *atkes*, those yummy potato pancakes fried in oil and eaten on Chanukah, create some of the liveliest, happiest, and noisiest days of the year. Although there are many things I would like to be remembered for, I fear that my neighbors know me best as *Maman*, the woman with the French name for mother, who sets off her smoke alarm. Very often.

Ingredients:

- Whatever potatoes you have around (unpeeled! – who has time?)
- 1 onion – shred until all eyes in room are sufficiently teared up

- 6 eggs – regardless of the number of potatoes used
- Some salt – if your blood pressure can handle it
- Oil – better pick up a few gallons

Dirctions:

Heat oil in frying pan.

Process as many potatoes as food processor will shred before sounding like it will *plotz*.

Add remaining ingredients.

Light menorahs and join family in singing loud and joyous blessings, along with traditional Chanukah songs.

When smoke alarm starts shrieking from forgotten hot oil in frying pan, open windows.

Put oil aside to ask rabbi if burnt oil can be used in menorah for the second night of Chanukah.

Heat new oil.

Answer phone. Talk to old friend whom you haven't heard from in many years.
(Ahhh...what a *shmooze!*)

Answer door and give chocolate coins and donuts to two men collecting donations for Israel.

When living room fills up with smoke, open doors along with windows.

Find kitchen through smog.

Put oil aside to be used (maybe?) on second night.

Give out mittens, hats and scarves to children who are freezing inside the cold house.

Heat more oil.

Read story of Chanukah to little ones while bigger ones listen on with renewed pleasure.

Pledge one box of chocolate coins to organization on phone.

When neighbor shows up to ask why smoke is coming through shared wall, invite them and family in for latkes and an animated round or two of Dreidel, a traditional game using a top with letters on all four sides.

Find kitchen and the now blackened frying pan.

Set oil aside to be used (maybe) on third night of Chanukah.

Give neighbor's children extra sweaters.

Heat more oil.

Finish turn at Dreidel and wrap now-frozen children in blankets.

Warm up large pot of hot cocoa.

When fire department arrives from smoke billowing out from open windows and doors, serve hot cocoa to firemen, see if any of them are Jewish, and have them light a menorah.

Put aside oil, hopefully to be used for the fourth night of Chanukah.

Heat more oil...

Nana Ruth, Passover and the Flowers That Kept on Coming

N ana Ruth, as she became affectionately known in our home, was coming for the Passover Seder.

Midday on Passover eve, in walked Nana Ruth, a trim, professional woman wearing a crisp, cream-colored suit with a matching clutch and perfectly coifed hair. Her coordinating pumps elegantly graced her movie star legs – legs that should have been insured by Lloyd's of London. Especially as they walked through *my* pre-Passover home.

I was mesmerized – and horrified – as I watched her carefully navigate the maze of books, toys, bags, vacuum hoses and children, all while balancing a beautiful bouquet of flowers in one hand. Finally, she arrived in our kitchen, which had been transformed into our Passover kitchen extraordinaire.

Ruth's eyes opened wide as she took in the scene. The room was draped with plastic, foil and bed sheets – to cover appliances that would not be needed. There were cases of fruits and vegetables piled about, and piles of peels on the floor. The kitchen resembled a cross between an operating room, a Mars rover and a barn.

A homemade stove was propped on top of the regular stove, which was covered with a sheet, looking like a ghost of its former self. There were children peeling potatoes onto large piles on the floor – a tradition born the year my husband thoughtfully and brilliantly built us a Passover stove, finishing two hours before the holiday. That year, we lined up the children, instructing them to peel as fast as they could, creating large piles of peels on the floor. The entertaining acrobatics of catching our balance while rushing by on the slippery peels, combined with the thrill of doing something otherwise forbidden, was so joyful, it became our cherished tradition, to create peel piles on the floor each Passover eve.

Ruth gracefully closed her jaw, and smiled. She handed us the flowers, wiped a child's nose, and turned on her heel to navigate her path back to the door.

Oy. I cringed. Would she really come back?

Nana Ruth did come back. And she brought her husband Herman with her.

We had a very lively Seder that night – Ruth, Herman, and our large, lively family. It would have been laughable if it weren't so embarrassing. With children and grape juice spilling everywhere, Ruth wiped spills and noses, while Herman sat as if watching a Ping Pong match, following the busyness of the children and smiling a smile that I could not read... or perhaps didn't want to.

I still remember the silence after they left, broken only by the voice of an older child: "*That'll* be a Passover Seder they'll never forget!"

Surprisingly, Nana Ruth and Herman came back the next year.

And the year after that.

And the one following that year as well.

In fact, much to my surprise, each Passover eve, Nana Ruth would appear, impeccably dressed, with her perfectly coiffed hair, to navigate her path to the kitchen to drop off her flowers. We never knew *what* she would catch us in the middle of: the little ones cleaning their toys in the tub and hallway; the older boys cleaning furniture on the lawn; or a loud choir of children singing Passover songs in nasal voices. But it was, for sure, a behind the scenes event we would likely have chosen not to share.

Each time she came for the Seder, I would breathe deeply, wondering why she came back. It's not as if she didn't have local family of her own that she could have joined for the Seder – family whom she could have sat comfortably with, at a first class table set with the finest linens, beautiful china and crystal, and polished silver. I could just see her with lots of polite throat clearing and proper chatter. Sure, we had cleaned up the peel piles and made a beautiful home before the Seder, with the children dressed in their holiday finest, seated at a pretty table covered with thick plastic. We had done away with real dishes early on, voting to have more people singing at the table than scrubbing at the sink. And as for our grandmother's fine silver – well, the year my husband searched four large black garbage bags in our dark alley for a fork, only to find it hidden in the dishrack, gave birth to the tradition of disposable utensils.

But Nana Ruth just kept coming back. She even came back the year one child took it upon herself to enforce our tradition of washing in age order, broadcasting each time we washed,

"NANA RUTH'S THE OLDEST – SHE GOES FIRST!"

Although Ruth was sophisticated, well-spoken and anything but shy, she never mentioned this slight. Or the peel piles. Or that she could hear us from the curb as she pulled up to deliver her flowers. Instead, she would watch the children with fascination and respect as they swept or vacuumed or did any other job she may have caught them at, and praised them for being involved and responsible and part of the family. She enjoyed how it was all a team effort. Ruth smiled as she watched the children haul piles of school-made *hagaddahs*, the guides for the Seder, to the table, so they could give lively words of Torah, making our Seder longer than anyone would be expected to sit for. Yet, Nana Ruth would sit, smile and wipe.

Each year, I marveled at the juxtaposition of our boisterous clan and this refined, elegant woman, who somehow looked joyfully relaxed in our lively chaos.

I grew to understand that our Seder, with its busyness and lack of elegance, had the love, joy and strength of traditions, with a promise of future generations continuing them, which was all very satisfying to Ruth. *That* was what she saw. And *that* was what drew her back year after year.

As for Herman, he continued coming with Ruth, watching the children spill, share words of Torah, sing... all the while following the action with that smile that I could not read, and was afraid to ask about. One year, after Herman was no longer alive, Nana Ruth confided in us that although she loved him dearly, Herman was somewhat of a sourpuss.

"Your Seder was the only time Herman ever smiled."

I got it. And I stopped cringing.

The Rebbe,
My Zaide

I must have been around eleven or twelve years old at the time. Our after school Hebrew class was making a trip into Crown Heights, the home of the Chabad-Lubavitch Chassidic community. There we would experience Shabbat – most of us for the first time.

Each of us was placed with a family for the weekend. It was all very different for us kids coming from more secular homes. The few details I remember: The mother had dark hair and was very beautiful; the family had many little children with one named Yossy; I slept in the front room where I could see through the win-

dow an old man next door in an overstuffed chair watching TV. All of the important things. I also remember delightful joy filled dancing with a group of girls to some 45 RPMs in a basement after Shabbat.

And I remember being in synagogue.

Looking down from the women's balcony, I was told, "If you look now, you will see The Rebbe." I looked down into the vast sea of men in dark suits, beards, black fedoras and prayer shawls – to a girl from a secular background, they *all* looked like Rebbes. And I was too shy and embarrassed to ask which one he was.

The Rebbe, as he is affectionately called, was not only the leader of this community, but one of the most influential rabbis of the 21st century, respected throughout the world as a great Torah scholar and leader. In 1978 the President of the United States proclaimed his birthday as "Education and Sharing Day USA", and it has since been proclaimed annually. The Rebbe's mission was to elevate every individual to his maximum potential. His unconditional love for all Jews no matter the label, affiliation or beliefs is shared by his *Shluchim*, emissaries, rabbis and their families that he sent to every corner of the world to search out every Jew and infuse within him a love for G-d. The Rebbe reached out to Jews and non-Jews, wealthy and poor, heads of state and simple people who needed guidance or a blessing. The amount of lives he influenced and continues to influence as his message is passed on to others is ongoing and universal.

Although a *chassid* is one who *follows* the teachings of a *Rebbe*, a teacher, The Rebbe did not create followers – he created leaders. Most chassidim, have their own special story about meeting The Rebbe. Some are about miracles, and others, more the over the fence type from people who lived in the community with him. There are stories of how he would send an envelope of money for a woman to purchase a wig to cover her hair in a beautiful and modest way. Personal stories that do not deny that The Rebbe was The Rebbe, but acknowledge that he was a beloved person in these people's lives, and they were cherished by him as well. As far as Rebbe stories go, mine is not the most sophisticated one. But it's mine.

My relationship with The Rebbe is also not very sophisticated. The Rebbe is my *Zaide*, my kind, warm and welcoming *yiddishe* grandfather. And like those mythical characters in the best Zaide stories, he is someone I turn to for warmth, advice and encouragement. And as with any Zaide, I love to visit.

When our children were young, we would pile everyone into the 15 passenger van and ride for hours from Pittsburgh to New York, pulling into the *Ohel* – the burial place of The Lubav-

itcher Rebbe – in the middle of the night. Because a soul is eternal, it is a tradition for Jewish
people to visit graves of family and righteous
people to request that they intervene on our be-
half. As far as the middle of the night – that was
our own tradition, to enjoy the quiet of this often busy destination.

Once at the Ohel, we would sit in the welcome center enjoying the cookies and milk our
Zaide had waiting for us. We would draw pic-
tures and write letters, telling The Rebbe about
our learning, our mitzvot, our accomplishments,
our hopes, dreams, disappointments, and challenges. While the children busied themselves
eating, writing, and running around, we would
drink in the feelings of *nachas,* pride, of a Zaide
for his grandchildren, and for us, for raising
them as chassidim.

Although we are blessed with devoted and
loving parents who cherish their grandchildren,
as Baal Teshuvah – those who have taken on a
Torah observant way of life – there are some
unique traditions that come along with being a
chassid that don't always translate well, and
perhaps are best not shared. For example, can
you picture calling your parents:

"Hello Mom, Dad… I know it's the middle of
the night, but we're in a cemetery, in the snow,
wearing slippers, making toasts, and singing
and dancing with a group of strangers in honor

of your grandson reciting a very long discourse in Yiddish at the graveside of a great Rebbe ... we though you might want to join us?" You can't do that to your parents. They love us. They worry. Our lives can be scary to them. Some of the things that we do share can be hard enough on them like the traditionally larger families we tend to have.

I remember calling home, 30 weeks pregnant: "Dad, remember that sonogram we were going to have? Dad, are you sitting down? We are having twins!"

Silence.

More silence.

Pregnant pause.

A very quiet, almost inaudible... "*Oy vey.*"

More silence.

A little throat clearing ... "That's ... really great... I'll ... be sure to tell Mom when she gets home."

Click.

Dad called back 10 minutes later to apologize: "I'm so sorry. That's really wonderful news. It's just that... all I kept thinking about was... *My poor baby!*"

I felt so loved. And I understood. Perhaps the four boys ages 1, 2, 4 and 6 years old playing in the background did make it seem a little over the top.

As our children continued to grow in numbers and knowledge, we continued to visit The Rebbe – in a somewhat more civilized manner, with bigger questions to ask and blessings to request. At some point one of the children informed us that the cookies and milk were actually there as a break-fast for those who kept the tradition of fasting before their visit to the Ohel. I suppose they could be used for that purpose as well.

It was a journey to truly comprehend who the Rebbe was. I remember learning of the Rebbe's stroke from the Shaliach we were close to at the time, who mentioned he was going to New York. I asked this emissary if he would be doing The Rebbe's work for him while he was recovering. His look told me that I truly did not understand who The Rebbe was, and by the time I did, special opportunities to visit with this very holy man for blessings in a private audience, or distribution of dollars for people to give to *tzedakah*, charity, were no longer an option. In fact, the next time I was in 770 Eastern Parkway, Chabad-Lubavitch World Headquarters after my Shabbat in Crown Heights was to bring my oldest son for his first time being called up to the Torah as a bar mitzvah.

Did I see The Rebbe that day when I visited 770 as a young girl? Possibly. Did The Rebbe see me? I would love to think that he did, and I often go to the back of the woman's section of the synagogue to try to recreate the same vantage point, hoping... I am not sure what, but it feels so good to just sit there.

What about all the many people who never did see The Rebbe – perhaps myself included?

None of our children has met The Rebbe, yet each of them has a personal relationship with him that is uniquely their own. We have brought each of them for their bar or bas mitzvah to the Ohel, to share that *nachas* with The Rebbe. I remember one child standing between us in his rubber sandals reciting a *ma'amar*, a traditional Yiddish discourse, as it snowed lightly. I quietly cried grateful tears for this moment I would never have dreamed of, and noticed snow dripping off The Rebbe's gravestone – surely his tears of *nachas* as well.

As these new generations come to the Ohel for blessings and *brachos*, cookies and milk, they are writing their own Rebbe stories, creating their own relationships as beautiful and meaningful and real as any chassid's of a previous generation, and uniquely their own. Each of us is a beloved chassid to the holy righteous *tzaddik*, and a precious grandchild to the *Zaide*.

I sat recently at the table in the Ohel, overwhelmed by the magnitude of the opportunity to be there, the amount I felt I should write, and the limited time in which to do so, and my brain froze. I looked up at one of our now grown sons and whispered, "I can't concentrate or write *anything*!" He comforted me: "Just write what comes to mind. Don't worry about it. He *is* The Rebbe ... but he's also someone who cares about you very much. He just wants to hear from us."

Somehow, I must have forgotten. He's my Zaide.

Just a
Moment of Peace

K*nock knock knock*, "Maman, do you know where the glubs are?"

Putting my makeup down on the counter to better concentrate on the cute little "fwee" year old on the other side of the door, I answered, "Sweetie, go and put on some pants. And then we can talk about gloves."

He didn't miss a beat: "Oh Maman, you're so funny – I don't want to *talk* about glubs, I want to *wear* them." I could hear the smile in his step as he walked away from the door.

As I critiqued my blush, I noticed little fingers wiggling under the door, and then a yellow plastic wrench was passed through the space. I was hoping I wouldn't need it for anything important, when my thoughts were interrupted by another customer: *tap tap tap*: "Maman, Do you know where my birth certificate is? I need it for a school trip."

"I don't see it in here," I continued through the door, "… but I'm happy to look for it when I come out."

"Maman, are you in there?" another, higher pitched voice inquired, "…can Estie sleep over tonight?"

Putting the cap back on my lipstick I answered, "Children, please. This is not an information booth. It's a bathroom. Five minutes. I am sure everything can wait for five minutes while I put on some makeup. And then we can solve all the problems of the world.

At least our little world.

Knock knock knock, "Maman… one of the white chickens was in the house and laid an egg in my bed."

"I'm coming out!"

I know that one day I will miss the rhythm, song and pungent odors of raising a large lively bunch of kids, and I consciously take moments to breathe it all in. But five minutes? Seriously.

When the children were younger I had my five minutes and more. There was naptime, and a 7:30 bedtime, which was my time to buzz around the house, my head deep in concentration while my body conquered its own to do list. I believed that as the children got older, time alone in the house would only become more plentiful. I'm not sure why I believed this. The reality has been varied schedules and obligations – many days I find myself inhaling, entering the "zone" as I watch the last person leave for the day, only to exhale moments later as someone comes through the door for the evening in an almost seamless do-si-do.

So began my quest to find a place for some uninterrupted time.

In my dream, this place would have a door. And perhaps a sweet little "Maman is working" note taped to the front of it. I knew just the place. I fabricated a desk in the only room that seemed practical: the laundry room. Who would want to be in there? I put photos on the walls to shift the focus from "how *much* laundry" to "the blessed *source* of all the laundry." It was perfect. It even had a door. Except that most of what I needed to do was on the other side of that door. And with the machines running most days, it was not necessarily conducive to quiet.

New ideas came and went, but ultimately, the place I found my five minutes of peace turned out to be in the middle of a busy room, in the middle of the day.

How could it be?

It all began a few hours before candle lighting on the 7th night of Passover when we got a call from the obstetrician. I was at the beginning of a pregnancy and he had insisted that I take a sonogram to be sure that I was not having twins again.

"I am so sorry to bother you," he said. He *never* calls. My heart began to race. "We got the results back from your sonogram. They were... irregular." He went on to explain the possibilities. Truly frightening.

I found my husband and shared the news. We agreed that Hashem was in charge and it would all be fine. We went back to what we were doing before the interruption.

Within minutes I was back at his side, panicked, searching his eyes for comfort, and the confidence of his words: "Really, it will all be OK." *Sephardim,* Jews from of Middle East and North African origin, know these things, and I had grown to count on him for that.

To secure the calm, he went to the bookshelf and pulled out a volume of letters from The Rebbe. He opened it randomly, falling on a letter that read something to the effect that "...where you used to live, women did not *daven*, recite the daily prayers. Where you live now, it is appropriate for you to learn."

I had honestly been dreading the day when my kids would be grown and I would no longer have the excuse of being too busy with little children to learn how to daven all the prayers in the prayer book. I called a Rebbetzen and made arrangements for her to teach me. Meanwhile, optimism replaced fear as we occupied ourselves with grabbing mitzvot and acts of kindness in the merit of our baby – going well beyond what was comfortable for two introverts.

I met with the Rebbetzen who started me off with the morning prayers, later adding prayers I was familiar with from my children's davening, and finally adding the big girl prayer: Shemona Esrei. We started with a small portion, taking three steps back, three steps forward, standing with feet together, facing east, towards Jerusalem, and my closet. I slowly read each word, trying not to get discouraged by how slowly I was going and how much more there was to learn.

I noticed how the children would walk quietly around me when I stood feet together facing the closet, "Maman?" one would ask, "Shhhhh" a sibling would answer, "She's davening." Children stepped in to help each other, diverted questions and answered requests. Sometimes I would take so long that I would leave deep footprints in the carpet, yet no matter what chaos reigned around me, they would not interrupt.

I had found my space, my door with the note, my crazy oasis of uninterrupted calm, and more...

This space is not empty.

When I take three steps back and three steps forward, G-d is there. It is just the two of us in His chamber. And I feel loved.

He wants to hear His favorite song, the big girl prayer which has become a salve for my day. There is a space for me to ask for things that I need, and request to heal those I love or don't even know. He wants me to remember that there is so much to be grateful for, and to get my mind into that song of gratitude. He wants to teach my children how to speak to their parents and friends by modeling the words in this prayer. He requests these words not for himself, but for me, as a reminder that He is there, that He holds it all – I merely need to dance my part.

In His embrace I can let go. The tension and worry won't change a thing. It is He who is in charge. He runs the world, and it is all according to a greater plan that I am too limited to comprehend. It may look like chaos from where I am standing, with life whirling around outside my little eye of the storm, but there is a plan. And He wants me to know this. He wants me to know that I am safe.

It's an opportunity to get my priorities back in order, to recharge, to hard reset, or even just to rest in my charging cradle. It's a time to smile and be held in His embrace, for Him to soothe and comfort His child, lifting the troubles of the world. At least my little world.

There really needs to be better PR about this davening thing – sure, it is a lot to do, but how can I complain? G-d wants to hear from me. He wants me to check in and to know how my day went, "So, what's new my child, what can I do for you?" For Him it's not an interruption.

Knock knock knock. "Maman, are you in there?"

"Who is it?" I put my lipstick down once more to enjoy the child on the other side of the door. That same child that we prayed so hard for:

As the moment came for the baby to be born, my husband stepped outside the delivery room to focus on prayers and allow me some privacy. Meanwhile, on the table, I panicked, grabbing the nurse's hand, nearly crushing her finger as the optimism and faith we nurtured all those months moved aside as thoughts of: "How will my world change?" filled my heart with fear.

Perhaps the phone call from the doctor was an opportunity to affect the outcome. We will never actually know. But we are beyond grateful for the healthy and whimsical child that G-d sent us. The one speaking through the door of my information booth:

"Maman, I just wanted to tell you that I love you."

The Great Parade

T he Great Parade. What an opportunity! With top performers, great food, and people coming to New York from all over to celebrate Lag BaOmer, a particularly joy filled day on the Jewish calendar, The Great Parade promised to be the event of the year.

Our youngest son was beyond excited to go. Two buses had been chartered from our school – one bus for the boy's school and one for the girl's school. Unfortunately, by the time my son was able to get a ticket, the boys' bus had sold out. The principal of the school assured my husband that he would keep us in mind in case a seat opened up.

On the morning before the parade, I received a call from my husband, "There was a cancellation! Can you go right away and pay for the seat?"

I ran over with my wallet and secured the dream! As I was leaving, I overheard the rabbi's secretary saying, "But Rabbi, the seat that canceled was on the girls' bus."

The rabbi answered, "It's no problem; we can just switch my parents from the boys' bus to the girls' bus." I was touched that the principal would move his parents to accommodate our son. The dream was still on.

Lag BaOmer day, the busses set out with great excitement. I was driving our 15 passenger van filled with high school girls for a separate celebration when I received a call from my son's chaperone. There had been an accident. He assured me that everyone was fine: "…many miracles… so many miracles!" I spoke to my son. Through the eyes of a ten year old, it was all a marvelous adventure. Comforted by my son's voice, I put the limited information I had received away, and continued on my way.

Later that evening, I was enjoying a lively bonfire at the girl's high school celebration when I received a call from the rabbi's niece. She and I had become close the previous summer when we accidently drove "down" the "up" ramp of a highway together, scaring ourselves out of our wits and bonding us forever. She called to tease me about our experience, as she often does, this time prompted by the news of the bus accident. She had heard that the driver who had caused the accident had been driving the wrong way on the highway, and she had to call. As we spoke further, I learned more details about the accident and how very serious it really was. I told her that my son just barely made it on that bus, and thanks only to the kindness of her uncle....

That's when it hit me: the rabbi's parents were supposed to be on that bus! What had been an exciting adventure for a ten year old boy could have been terrible for the principal's parents. I was grateful, and shaken. I had to call their daughter, the principal's sister, and my dear friend.

"It does not stop there" she said. "Not only would our parents have been on the bus that crashed, but they would have been sitting where they always sit, in the front seat – the seat where the only seriously injured person was sitting."

"Well, you paid her back", were her next words. "Don't you remember?"

Earlier that year, my friend's grandmother had passed away. We had been talking one night about how incredibly indebted I felt to her grandmother. So many of her children and grandchildren had been key influences in our family's growth, raising us up to a life of Torah observance, and attaching us to The Rebbe.

First it was my friend, her granddaughter, who made us into family. Then her grandmother's son, the rabbi of the community we had moved to, who nurtured us to the next level, *shlepping* us into New York to buy a frock coat for my husband, black fedoras for my husband and bar mitzvah age son, to visit the Ohel, and a stop at Kingston pizza. Her grandson, the principal, has kept an eye out for our boys, guiding them through high school and beyond. And all along our path, her grandmother's daughter and son-in-law, the principal's parents, have nurtured us like family.

I had told my friend that night on the phone, "I wish I could do something to repay your grandmother for all of the influence her children have had in our lives."

"You just did."

The Nugget that Saved Passover

A s I spin this tale about the women of the Tuesday morning women's class, please know that as with most legends, this one too is based on a true story. However, the names and details have been altered to protect both the privacy of those involved, and our friendships. At Passover time, we tend to go overboard cleaning the house of chometz, all leavened foods, and often get sidetracked and overambitious. Also know that all suggestions have been kid tested and approved, but could cause major damage to your home or contents. Please check with your homeowner's insurance and a qualified rabbi before attempting any of the following suggestions.

The room filled with the heavy scent of overly sweetened and clashing perfumes as the women of the Tuesday Morning women's class noisily assembled around the table to *kvetch, nosh* and learn a little.

As the mavens of homemaking un-burped Tupperware of leftover *kugel* and un-foiled plates of mandelbrot, Jewish biscotti, they listened as Faiga Markowitz* filled their imaginations with visions of her Grand *Geuladik* Passover Resort Vacation, with an extra emphasis on the *Geula*, redemption. Yes, this year, she was truly going to be in Jerusalem. OK, so it wasn't *actually* Jerusalem. It was Miami. But redemption is redemption, and not needing to clean her stylishly over cluttered house for Passover was as sweet a liberation as Faiga could ever have prayed for.

The women sighed as they imagined lavish kosher for Passover meals expertly prepared for and served to Faiga's large and rather charismatic family, while she sat regally and, oddly enough, awake at the Seder.

While Faiga Markowitz sat exuding an air of calm and joy, the overtired women of the Tuesday Morning class shared *their* pre-Passover images. They had been scrubbing, sorting, and disassembling their homes, along with the lives of everyone around them. Adelle had taken down all the curtains, Rochel had repainted and Becky had retiled. Meanwhile, Rose had foiled her kitchen until it looked like a NASA landing module, and Devorah had been serving dinner in the basement since Chanukah. They discussed carpet cleaners, dry cleaners, and oven cleaners used in ways the manufacturer would *not* have suggested or endorsed. All the while, the women passed pieces of biscotti with scrunched up noses, whispering *"chametz"*, as if they were passing dead mice by their tails. It was a scary scene.

And as Passover drew closer, it only got worse.

The women scoured, while Faiga dreamed. The women sanded and plastered, while Faiga dreamed. They scraped and boiled, torched and foiled, while Faiga...PANICKED – three days before the holiday was to begin, her Grand *Geuladik* Passover Resort Vacation was cancelled. The women shopped, while Faiga phoned the rabbi.

After an intense war room style consultation, Faiga Markowitz reappeared looking disheveled and *ah shtickle farshvitzt*, (untranslatable but much as it sounds) armed with a nugget of wisdom and strength from the rabbi. With no spring cleaning added on, no home repairs squeezed in, with the size 5 trousers left in her size 7 son's dresser and only the Passover laws and customs observed, the Markowitz family could very well pull this off.

Ever generous, Faiga shared her powerful nugget with the weary women of the Tuesday Morning class: "Ladies, we are commanded to learn the laws of Passover 30 days before the holiday. This refreshes our memories, and helps us separate law and customs – from spring cleaning and *mishugas*."

The women's shoulders sagged lower as she continued, "Those 30 days, when we do the bulk of our cleaning and shopping, fall in the Jewish month of Adar – when we are commanded to be joyous. My friends," she concluded, "perhaps G-d is telling us something: We must be careful when we sweep out the crumbs for Passover that we *do not* sweep out the joy of Adar."

Not a sound was heard. Jolted from their self-imposed exiles the women were shocked to hear how few of their ambitious preparations were actually necessary, and remorseful of the toil and rigor they had imposed on their families. With their newfound perspective, and a sparkle in their eyes, the women repented, rethought their Passover preparations, went home, and got to work:

Becky, ever the maven of efficiency, *schlepped* a large dry-erase board to her dining room table, breaching the caution tape that cordoned off the area like a crime scene. She listed the jobs yet to be accomplished and invited her family up from the basement to discuss the new goals, quotas, and incentives.

Meanwhile, from the sidewalk outside Rochel's house, you could hear music, vacuuming, and the nasal voices of older children mimicking Passover story tapes. One door over, lined up in neat military rows on the front lawn, was Rose's furniture. Having older boys, she used her Mars/Venus techniques, asking them if they "would" help, then gave them the space to clean the way boys do – using the garden hose. From the upstairs window of the next house came the sounds of young voices laughing and splashing – it was Devora's children *"kashering"* their toys using more enthusiasm and water than the hallway carpet could possibly hold.

Adele called her husband Sam, who had taken up residence at the park, and asked him to "please come home... and do bring the children." She gave them all peelers, and looked the other way, as they peeled *everything* – an honored family tradition. How fun it was to try to hold a peeled watermelon and, *oh,* the aerobic antics a floor full of peels provides.

But the *chayus*, the extreme exuberance, did not stop there – oh no...

Faiga Markowitz was unstoppable with that nugget. With her new perspective on Passover cleaning, she was actually delighted to be home for the holiday. In fact, she went all out – actually permitting the long banished school-crafted *Haggadahs,* with their tiny hand towel swatches and cupcake-paper Seder plates to be brought to the table. She gave her guests slave duds, and plague props – which was embarrassing of course – but everyone had to agree that the mirrored sunglasses for the plague of darkness were very cool.

She sent *all* the children to open the door for Elijah the prophet while Yossel, infected with her playful and light hearted mood, quickly donned a white sheet and a staff, reaching for the cup of Elijah as they all returned. Absolutely awe-inspiring – although, *ah shtickel* creepy. Together, they encouraged, words of Torah, songs, and skits – *Rabbi Elazar ben Azariah* style – 'until the time came for reciting the morning prayers.' This did not make them popular with their guests, but what a *chayus* it created for the children.

As for the women of the class, the Tuesday morning after the Sederim, bright and early, the room filled with the distinctive scent of kosher for Passover dish soap, as the women noisily assembled around the foiled table to reflect upon their Passover adventures. They all had to agree – the rabbi had changed the holiday for them forever with his powerful nugget of wis-

dom and strength. Although they had enthusiastically given up much to prepare Passover,
they were grateful to have their sanity and the
company of their families back. The women
found great value being as strict with Adar joy
as they had been with Passover crumbs, and
they loved the sweet memories and new traditions their families had created.

After all, the Seder is about the children: their
curiosity, keeping them awake, telling over the
story of the exodus from Egypt, and ultimately,
having them dream big colorful dreams of their
own lively Sederim, and the joy filled lively
wacky over-the-top preparations that go into
creating them. May they inspire the generations
to come and journey with them to the final redemption, which promises to be even more
wonderful than Miami.

Dear Editor,

I would like to personally thank those of you who have led me on the path to enlightenment regarding healthy living. May it bring a blessing of health into your lives.

And to the editors of magazines, such as yours, that print recipes for nontoxic home cleansers, may you be blessed with harmony and balance.

And to my family, who has embraced this change in our home, may you always have the blessing of acceptance in your own lives.

And to my dear husband, who graciously called the rabbi after we realized that the vine-

gar that my enlightened self had innocently instructed the family to use for Passover cleaning
is made of grain, which may not be used for
Passover, may you have the continued blessing
of serenity, humor and forgiveness.

And to my children who had just wiped the
dining room chairs, tables, and assorted other
surfaces throughout our home ... for the third
time... may it be an atonement, and may Passover always go smoothly in your own homes.

And to anyone reading this, I wish for you
the great blessing of learning from others' mis-
takes.

Wishing everyone a happy and kosher Passover.

Chana Gittle Deray
Pittsburgh, PA

Mr. Magoo or Mrs. Deray

I went brown water rafting today! I certainly hadn't planned on it. It is all quite a miracle. *Baruch Hashem*, thank G-d, I am home with only a bump, a scrape, two splinters... and maybe a little wisdom.

I was returning home from a shopping trip in my big old red 15 passenger van. I was alone, enjoying a breathtaking Pittsburgh downpour, complete with thunder, lightning and hail. Visibility was very limited, but curiously, I felt safe and was enjoying the challenge. The rain was amazing in its volume and beauty! I even rolled

down the window to admire it further.

Traffic was moving very slowly as we followed closely behind each other's vehicles. All of a sudden, I saw nothing but a cascade of rain through my windshield. Stopping, I felt something hit the van. A tree had come down on the car next to mine, and must have hit my van as well. The man looked startled but otherwise fine. I started to panic. The entire area was thick with trees. I drove over something which only added to my uneasiness. I needed to get somewhere safe. I noticed a police station ahead, and pulled in.

As I was telling the officer about the downed tree, in ran another officer. "Get all the keys! We need to move the cars! The manhole cover in the parking lot just blew and water is shooting up like a geyser!" The parking lot was flooding quickly. The officer asked me to "move *that* van!" Not knowing where to go, I got in and back on the road.

I had only driven a short distance when everything stopped moving. With the outer lanes flooded, all traffic was in the center lanes. Looking ahead, I could see another geyser. And then water started coming down the street in a small wave. The water around us began to rise very quickly. I pulled the van higher up, onto the wide divider. I was terribly frightened, imagining the water continuing to rise at this rate.

I grabbed my purse and got out, yelling to the woman whose car was facing mine to get out. Thinking that everyone else was crazy to just sit there in the rising water, I decided to cross the current, hoping to get to the higher ground while the water was still low enough to deal with.

The current was quite forceful but I was holding strong, making my way across. About halfway there, the water pulled me in, knocked me down and began carrying me down the street, which was at this point like a rushing river. I don't remember if I said it to myself or out loud, but my thought was clear: "I am not dying today!"

I started digging my heels into the pavement beneath the water. The current was so powerful that my efforts seemed to have no effect. Somehow I moved to the side enough that the ground below me was now grass. I turned myself over and attempted to dig my fingers into the ground, hoping to stop myself from being dragged along. It slowed me down enough that I was able to pull myself out of the current and crawl to the side.

I pushed myself through a row of bushes and stood up. I was overcome with the terrifying feeling of not knowing where to find safety. I was shaken, my foot was bleeding, and my clothes were soaked and filled with bits of leaves and sediment. Somehow, my *sheitel*, my hair covering was still on, *Baruch Hashem*. G-d is so kind.

A police officer approached and offered to take me by truck to the police station. He said that the water would draw back soon, so I decided to stay near the bushes so that I could dash to my van as soon as the water receded. I stood there thanking Hashem, calming and centering myself with prayer.

The water finally did recede. The officers pushed the flood damaged cars off the road. Still shaken, I went to my van and slowly started driving home. I passed blown out manhole covers, scattered like large coins on the now deserted road. I debated whether to give in to drama. Nope, not going there. It happened, and Thank G-d I am fine. I drove and talked to myself to stay calm. "I saved the big old red van!" "Okay, I know that Hashem saved the van, but I get one point for pulling it up on to the divider!"

At home, I was gracefully told by my son that the best action would have been to stay in the van with the window open so that I could get out, possibly going up on the roof if I needed to. I felt somewhat foolish, even with my one point for saving the van. (In a cheap attempt to save my dignity here, I would like to note that the news reported that the water rose to five feet high, leaving people screaming in their cars, not knowing whether to stay put or get out. I am horrified to further add that one month later, on this same street, the scene repeated itself. This time the water rose to ten feet, resulting in the deaths of two women and two girls. Three of them were trapped in their car.)

What was that all about? What was Hashem trying to tell me? All of us? I called a good friend to see if she could help me sort it out. It turns out, she was actually visiting her parents in Pittsburgh and had been standing on their porch watching the storm. She usually takes great pleasure in doing this, but the severity of this storm shook her up. She asked G-d to please protect anyone out driving in such a rain and then went inside, unable to bear watching any longer. We marveled at the Divine Providence. We felt the warm feeling of our connection to each other, and to Hashem. I thanked her for her prayers. Together we laughed that her prayers should have been for someone swimming in that rain, not driving.

It was later that evening when I understood the truths.

I was giving my husband some cooking spoons I had picked up for him while shopping. "Sorry I didn't wrap them... I had planned to but... I had kind of a hectic day!"

Isn't this how my days always go? I am never really in control. I just don't always get to see it this clearly. I go along with life making choices, but in reality I am on Hashem's chartered course. I am only safe each moment because He has total control. I may think it is because I am digging in my heels, and I better continue to do so, but that is not what keeps me safe. In a life filled with endless situations and decisions, I don't always see the dangers or consequences. Yet, more often than I realize, I am saved from them.

I remember a little cartoon I used to watch growing up called Mr. Magoo. He was this absolutely distracted, possibly blind, cheery little old man with two lines for eyes. The cartoon would open with Mr. Magoo walking to work. He would unknowingly walk into a construction site and be saved from falling into a ditch by a beam that was being lifted by a crane. He would continue walking from one beam to the next, totally unaware that he was up in the air. As he continued, one beam would seamlessly intersect the next. This would continue until he would miraculously arrive at work, without a scratch or any knowledge of what had happened.

Isn't this how my days go?

This is also why my life has any value, meaning, or purpose. I could never make a plan for a life that would actually add up to something! I am not that wise. Hashem will take care of me, giving me the challenges I need to make my life one of meaning and value, taking me to the edge of what I think I can handle, pushing me a little further than I would ever choose to go, then pulling me back before I break or, heaven forbid, drown. He is truly in charge. I can, however, make decisions of how I will deal with all these situations: honestly, decently, with integrity… the way Hashem would want me to.

Later that night there was another storm, and the fear came back. I was frightened by what had happened, the terrifying feeling of not knowing where to find safety, and even more, that I could not even say that I knew what I would do if I were ever in such a situation again. Of course, at that hour, the fear spread to all areas of my life. I panicked about the safety of our children who were working and participating in camps in many places. How can we feel any sense of control over what will happen to them? We can educate them, give them "the safety talk," but ultimately, it is not in our hands. It's not even in our hands when they are babies and literally in our hands! I am totally not in control. Never have been. Not out there today, not any other day past or future. Hashem is in charge. These were the thoughts that ultimately comforted me, and allowed me to go back to sleep.

Now that some time has passed, I have to say that I am truly grateful for this experience. First of all, I would never have chosen to do anything that cool. I am more the type to struggle with the standard white water rafting disclaimer of life and limb, and I would gladly accept a helmet and airbags, if they would be offered. Only Hashem could have gotten me into this situation.

Although I had no doubt that Hashem is in charge, seeing so vividly what that truly means has influenced how I view so many situations. I have learned to yield more to Hashem the power that I never had in the first place. I can also better accept that, hey, that's just the way He wants it to be. And this is truly what is best. It is a great relief to let go of being both me and G-d.

I will leave you with a blessing that all of your challenges be meaningful, purposeful, and... cool! May you face them all with strength, clarity, and a life vest... one that is securely fastened to Hashem's loving hand!

Married To a Gardener

R unning late as usual, I hopped into my big old 15 passenger van and took off for the babysitter's house. The uniquely familiar odor filling the van hit me right away. Maybe if I rode with the windows open, the babysitter would never need to know what was causing that pungent smell.

Such are the quandaries that marriage has introduced into my life – specifically, being married to a gardener. It's a life filled with . . . wonderment, and at that moment I needed to cherish each wonder, as I gracefully explained to the babysitter why there were 500 pounds of manure in the back of my van. Her expression revealed that she had not yet cultivated a sophistication for such finery, but alas, she was still young. I too once believed that green beans grew from cans, and strawberries from the freezer. At the very least, she would appreciate the extra weight smoothing the ride home as our old van rumbled over the bumps and potholes.

Gardeners are just not ordinary people. They note the change in seasons by the arrival of summer and winter seed catalogs; they measure property sizes by possible tomato yields; they live in growing zones instead of states; and they have an uncanny sense of always knowing when it's going to rain – regardless of the weather outside.

My introduction to the gardening way of life came shortly after the *chupah*, the canopy a couple stands under, symbolizing the creation of their home and life together. In a slow, almost ceremonial manner to accommodate its extreme mass, my new husband moved a bark-covered, moss-enhanced wooden planter type structure into our apartment. At the time, I did not realize the significance of this event. Looking back now, I see that it rivaled the *chupah* in its symbolism and sanctity – except that under the chupah I prayed that our life together would last for an eternity, and upon seeing his planter, I petitioned the heavens that the half-life of wood and bark was not very long. It was a little concerning, but I was aware as a young bride that men can be a little quirky.

Thankfully, our life together blossomed, while the moss and bark decomposed. Naively, I thought that would be the end of it – until years later, when I stepped out of our apartment to where a small neglected patch of sand, dirt and rocks once sat. In its place there was lush green foliage, with chubby little boys sitting and munching green beans! Yes, I knew about our chubby little guys – but I could never have imagined that beans grew from the ground of all places, and how extraordinary they could taste.

As the children grew in size and number, so did the gardens. From the window of our first home, I looked out one day to find my husband with a band saw in hand, his *tzitzit* – a fringed undergarment reminding him of the 613 commandments – with its strings flailing wildly, while trees fell in all directions. This offered a great deal of excitement for the children, and ample opportunity for heartfelt prayer for me. He set the children up with their own gardens and worked with them to grow their plants. They saved the first fruits and vegetables of each crop for Shabbat, and beamed when they found them in the meal. We even had berries for dessert, and fresh flowers on the table… as long as our little farmers didn't lovingly drown them.

The children learned to save seeds from whatever they were eating: melon, peppers, apples. I once watched as chubby, hope filled fingers extracted the "seeds" from a cone of chocolate chip ice cream – precious!

The children took their passion for planting with them to yeshivahs and camps, growing seeds on top of their bureaus and behind kitchens. They shared their enthusiasm and results with their father in phone conversations meant only for those on the inside: "Really? Asian pears in zone 5? Amazing! Great job!"

What I had not realized was that along with that bark-covered atrocity, this crazy, wonderful gardener had brought something magical into our lives. He brought a simple faith that if you stick a seed into the ground, something wonderful will grow.

This quality spilled out of the garden into many places of our life together: the courage to start businesses; the audacity to have an unacceptable amount of children; the conviction to raise them Torah observant; and the moxie to drive long distances with them all. It was a faith that I grew to depend on: when he planted seeds, it would always seem to rain, and when he said everything would be okay, it calmed my fears and restored my faith. This ingredient was not only for growing vegetables, but essential for success in anything we would do.

The Rebbe says "Think good, and it will be good." My mentor taught me that this means: "Our *believing* that G-d will make it good, *can* make it good." Our thoughts create the healthy soil for good to grow in. She explained further: "We are *commanded* to trust that G-d *will* make it good. And we must believe deeply. When we worry, we doubt G-d's ability. G-d is a loving father; He *will* take care of us." She even comforted me by mentioning that this did not come easily. "Faith is a service, and we must work at it."

There are things about being married to a gardener that still take some getting used to – like the uncanny way it rains on cue, and the uncertainty of never knowing *what* I will find inside our van. While most of our city neighbors work tirelessly to maintain their beautiful lawns, ours is almost gone – replaced by the awe on the face of a child pulling up a rutabaga, and the wonder of harvesting fresh potatoes where saggy ones were pushed into the ground. Through the miracles happening on the once-lawn, I am reminded that "thinking good" *creates* the healthy soil that "good" grows in, and that I must work hard on strengthening my own faith.

I have watched G-d fulfill the faith of the gardener, who taught me that if you put a seed into the ground, something wonderful will grow.

Perhaps a special place should be established under the chupah… to put a planter.

Total Immersion: The Only Way to Learn a Language

Although I have been married for many years to a man from Paris, my French remains as much a form of entertainment as it is communication. As my brother-in-laws like to tease, *"Tu parles Francais comme une vache Espagnole* – You speak French like a Spanish cow."* This is apparently very funny... if you are French.

I had actually taken French while studying in Montreal, which my husband equates with learning Spanish while living in England. How-

ever, my teacher – a gentle older woman, was so mesmerizing that I never quite got the concept of masculine and feminine words, for when she spoke, it was decidedly *all* female. And who in the world, other than G-d, would ever have imagined that I would marry a man from France?

Using my bovine French, and the language of smiles, I struggled hard to communicate with my new family. We celebrated the realization that *Coca Cola* is the same in both languages, sprinkling it plentifully throughout our dinner-time non-conversations: "Ahhh!..*Coca Cola*", "Oiu!... *Coca Cola*" , "Umm, *Coca cola*...."

But I needed more.

I started gathering French words and phrases from my husband's conversations, carefully stitching them together and rehearsing them until I was armed and ready to connect.

Joining my husband and his father for a traditional French breakfast, I greeted them with my primed parlance. My husband looked up at me in shock – obviously impressed – while my father-in-law quietly raised his newspaper higher, so that we could no longer see him. Leaning towards me, my husband gently whispered:

"Don't ever say that again."

I whispered back: "What did I say?"

Long silence.

Smiling uncomfortably, yet reassuringly he answered, "Just don't ever say that again."

He has yet to divulge the translation.

Language may not be one of my gifts, but it seemed a lost opportunity if our children were not bilingual. Being the parent at home, it was up to me to make that happen. My husband patiently instructed me, penciling translations into story books: "*Mais pas des elephants*" (but no elephants) I would read at bedtime. He even worked with me on my accent: "*Peu*," "No, *Peu*," "it's *peu*, not *peu*," "like this, *peu*," "not quite... *peu*"... and with great compassion, he accepted the fact that I may likely never hear the difference.

Each not-so-flowing syllable was hard earned, as my husband decided that the only way I would truly learn French was how he learned to speak English: total immersion – we would speak only in French. Although this made for many quiet evenings, our first four children spoke French as their first language. Albeit a new dialect.

We once hosted a Parisian whose rhythmic phrases flowed so eloquently that I *clearly* could not let her hear *my* French. But as little boys would have it, I found myself quietly disciplining one as she gushed with delight: "It's so *wonderful* that you speak to your children in *Hebrew!*"

Alas.

Linguistically challenged and all, I was recently thrust into another immersion program – this time by G-d. The new language is so powerful, that it penetrates your bones and cells. It becomes a dialogue and rhythm that hums in the background of your life, defining the way you see and breathe. The language is *bitachon:* a deep confidence that it is all from G-d, and that He wants it to be good.

It was one of those follow-up calls after a doctor's appointment. "We need to run a few more tests." You know the kind: you sit there frozen, heavy, unable to move or even put down the phone. Time stops, the room tilts, your mouth dries and your body fills with chemicals. You are thrust into another reality.

Your day becomes surreal, as if you're in an alternate timeline, separate from your surroundings. You are unable to wrap your head around anything for more than a few seconds. Worry and uncertainty consume your entire being as you cycle possible outcomes in an endless loop. The clock no longer matters. It is no longer about what everyone expects, it's just you and your Creator. Life from then on has a refreshing truth filled quality to it, like a deck of cards being tapped on a table, your priorities fall easily into place. Nothing is more important than staring at your husband and children: "How delightful is his smile; how hard she tries; how grateful I am...." All that overwhelmed you moments before, you now see as a privilege, and you beg, "Please G-d, allow me to do this forever."

In essence, what we have received is a call from our Father who longs to hear from us, "Please visit, it's been too long, I miss our conversations and closeness." We have been given the perfect opportunity to learn bitachon, because no matter how strong those around you are, there are ways that no one can help. It's as if He is saying, "There is only Me. I am here. Reach out for Me. I will catch you."

During the month of Tishrei I had tried hard to reboot my connection with G-d, but my regular methods all felt sluggish. I knew that phone call was to be my antidote. Holding on to that thought, however, was like holding on to a root while my body dangled over a cliff, becoming more challenging as time went on.

Worried? Not me. I was terrified. What was Hashem trying to say tell me? How would *I* possibly know! I can't even understand French.

I stitched together the little bitachon I could with support from family and friends, and semi-gracefully got through the first round of procedures and results. But I needed more. *I* needed a twelve-step-break-myself-of-worry program. I had become so fluent in the language of woe, giving worry such a kick, that a happy occasion could resemble a crisis.

I spent nights learning about bitachon – "Think good, it will be good" – and began to see clearly how I control my thoughts, feelings, and outcomes. I learned that each test, medical or otherwise, each breath, each day...it is all unknown. Worry depletes our energy, life and joy. But, we are able to shift out of fear at any given moment by changing our thoughts and inner dialogue. Worry is a choice.

As I began using the language of bitachon, I saw life begin to shift. Gathering all the positive energy I could muster, I waited for tests and results, praising G-d that the medical world does not yet rest during the lesser known Jewish holidays – or our many Chassidic ones.

When I lost my grip, I gathered the children and hung party decorations, celebrating the good outcome we would surely share. "I've got it, Hashem! Faith and joy is the way to serve You!" I thought I was championing!

Until that Friday. "It seems that I've missed you," said the doctor's message. "We'll go over *everything* on Tuesday." Only G-d could have choreographed it that in that one moment when I put the phone down, the doctor would call.

"Tuesday! How could I possibly cope until Tuesday?!" I studied every nuance in the recording, listening to it over and over again. What exactly did the doctor mean?

Why did Hashem want me to wait four more days? What did He want of me? Truly,… did I want to hear the results before Shabbat? No. I am a real baby. I would be fine if I never heard them.

When the monsoon of terror passed, I found myself sitting peacefully on a sand bar. Whatever the doctor says on Tuesday, it will be fine. Hashem has given me an enormous ability to cope. He is there. He will catch me. Maybe I'm not such a baby after all.

I then added *chutzpah* to my arsenal. I composed a list of the reasons Hashem should bless me with long life. I started feeling strong, peaceful… even joyful… oddly similar to times when… there was a joyful occasion. And there was! I was speaking the language of bitachon – it had reached my bones, my cells, it was becoming a dialogue and a rhythm that hummed in the background of my life, defining the way I saw and breathed. It was absolutely life giving to speak bitachon those four days. Life felt clear, joyful… the room shifted back, my mouth moistened, and the right chemicals started flowing through my body again.

Tuesday came. Along with the results. All was fine, *Baruch Hashem*!

I will probably continue to blunder in French, offering my brother-in-law a chicken (*poulet*, ignore the "t") instead of a sweater (*pull)* on a cold day, but – *pardon my French* – to me they both sound the same. But bitachon – now there's a language worth breaking your teeth over. With its strengthening dialogue playing a song of confidence in the background of our lives, bitachon connects us to our Father, who only wants to give us good. Armed with bitachon, we can finally break free of the confines of the worry ghetto, opening gates for worlds of good to come into our lives.

The Annual
Purim Treat

Y ou really meant well!
         You started off Purim morning, the
         most joyfully celebrated Jewish holiday on
the calendar, with half a grapefruit and some
rye toast.

You had half an avocado and tuna with no
mayo for lunch.

At around 2:00, your best friend delivered a
shalach manos, a traditional Purim basket of
goodies, with candy, pastries, fruit, cheese and
all imaginable delicacies.

You were very good... You put it on top of the
fridge.

At 2:07, you gave yourself permission to have a little piece of cake. It is Purim, after all, and it's a mitzvah to be joyful and celebrate.

At 2:09, you felt it was important to really celebrate, and you finished it off. In fact, you decided to be truly pious, fulfilling the commandment to be joyful and celebrate, and tasted the chocolate rum balls as well; after all, they were homemade by your friend who loves you and only wants the best for you. So you ate all of them.

At 2:18, the rest of your baskets started calling to you...

By 4:00, you had conducted your own personal taste test to see whose cookie pops were truly the best, cleansing your palate between tastes with some candy corn.

At 4:30, while clearing the table for the Purim meal, you found a few pieces of saltwater taffy that were not needed for packing gift baskets after all, and enjoyed this exclusive Purim treat, feeling very good for involving yourself so wholeheartedly in the holiday.

At 5:00, while your husband delivered the baskets with the kids, you finally had a chance to sit down. You decided the most important thing you could do for your family was to make for them a happy mother. You put your feet up, and had a cup of tea... with the French bread and the camembert cheese from an organization you support... and finished off the chocolate bar you started earlier... along with a tomato, for fiber and good conscience.

And now, at 6:00, with everyone enjoying the wonderful meal, you gracefully enjoy your salad and sliced eggs with no mayo. Your husband glances over at you with that look of pride, knowing exactly what you've been up to, glad that you've enjoyed your annual Purim treat and are now back to yourself... and even left him a few morsels of chocolate.

We Are
Those Women

I had been feeling like the thrill was gone. There just wasn't the same... passion there used to be. Our children were actually finding things in their lives that were more exciting than cleaning a playroom... or a chicken.

Visions of preparing Shabbat or Passover sans kid-power haunted my thoughts, inspiring feelings of loneliness and embitterment. Whew. Not pretty.

What happened to the days of scrubbing alongside multiple sets of chubby little hands as they washed tubs, sinks, and younger siblings in distracted moments? Fisher price had no edge over the Municipal Water Authority, with a pre-Passover bathtub overflowing with toys and bubbles becoming our tradition, along with the Sea of Reeds and soggy children that it produced. Granted, things were often carried out with a bit more water and enthusiasm than the manufacturer's recommendations, but the time together and feelings of success... simply delicious.

I took a deep cleansing breath. Anyone who actually believes the Lamaze techniques are for labor and delivery is missing their greatness. They are there to help you through life once your blessings have arrived. There is something to all of that breathe-don't-scream methodology.

Upon deeper reflection of my non-reflecting surfaces, I uncovered the real dirt in the matter. Although I may enjoy standing with my hands in a sink of warm sudsy water – transporting myself in a trance like a Chassidic master to exciting worlds beyond my dish rack – our children are growing up. Those chubby little hands are now the hands of young men getting other men to put on tefillin. They are the graceful hands of young women leading choirs, and performing skits. Perhaps in comparison, cleaning their rooms could be a little… lackluster?

This captain was not about to go down with her ship.

They're good kids. No – they're *great* kids, *Baruch Hashem*! – Thank G-d! They're just not feeling inspired right now. Not doing the dishes with the same spiritual devotion. Not holding to the same level of strictness with the laws of vacuuming. How could I bring them back to a higher spiritual place in their mopping?

I wonder what those women would do? Those extraordinary women whose image I have carried with me as the embodiment of feminine strength and wisdom. The Jewish women who saved our entire nation in Egypt.

It could not have been a darker time in our history. With faith and fortitude, the Jewish women crafted musical instruments with which to sing and dance when the day of our redemption would finally arrive. And until that day, they used all their talents – all their strengths, and gifts, to inspire their husbands to go on. Each woman with the wisdom of what her own husband needed in order to be raised back up. These women even convinced their husbands to bring more children into a world that seemed to nurture only darkness. It is only because of their vision and strength that we are even here today... albeit with shmears and dust balls.

What would those remarkable women do with an uninspired cleaning crew? Why, they would craft something delightful and... unexpected! They would enchant – get a little lively with it.

I turned my computer on and braced myself with a few chapters of Psalms. First job to tackle: the girl's room. I will send them an email:

~ ~ ~

BS"D

I was just upstairs, dusting fan lamps 😳 ... when I opened the door to your bedroom 😨. I was so taken 😮 by the piles of clothes, that I just started to

cry 😭. So filled with pride at the generosity 😊 , the thoughtfulness 😌, the determination 😤 to collect all that clothing for the survivors of the Virginia earthquake 😥... the one that, statewide, knocked over a total of 4 lawn chairs... that I had to write and tell you. I so wanted to be a part of this most selfless and worthwhile endeavor, that I have called the donation truck 🚚. I told them how not only had my precious daughters 😊 😊 collected enough clothing to clothe ALL of the poor and unfortunate female victims, but they 😊 😊 had sorted them into nice little piles. There were stockings. And plenty of white shirts. And school uniform skirts enough to start a marching band 😊. They were most grateful and will be

*sending the truck around four o'clock. They are
also working on a monument 😵 to be placed by
the Vietnam Veterans Memorial 😩 of a bronze
mountain of clothing in your honor 😵😖.*
   Now...can we get that laundry done 😠 !?

~ ~ ~

I hit "send" and waited for the medicine to
take effect. I noticed activity in their room that
evening. Baskets going down to the basement,
bags coming up. They smiled at me as they
passed by, and thanked me for the email. *Baruch
Hashem.* Life is good!

Now... to motivate their brothers downstairs.

I took another deep cleansing breath...
glanced at a copy of *Men are from Mars...* and
grabbed a book of Torah studies... for added
support. And that's where I found it – a super-
powered nugget of strength: "The Rebbe has
told us that according to Torah sources, the generation of the final Redemption will be a rein-
carnation of the generation that left Egypt."
That means that we *are* those amazing women!
We have the inner wisdom to inspire... to raise
up our families – it's in our bones, our DNA –
it's what we are made of.

 I took this new nugget of strength with me to
my computer, and got back to work, sending the
following email:

BS"D

NAME OF FACILITY: THE BASEMENT EX-
ECUTIVE SUITE, PGH, PA

<u>NOTICE OF REVOCATION OF FACILITIES
UNDER SECTION 374 OF THE PROPER
MAINTENANCE PROCEDURES CODE:</u>

IT HAS COME TO THE ATTENTION OF
THE AFOREMENTIONED ESTABLISH-
MENT THAT SO-NAMED OCCUPANTS
HAVE BEEN GROSSLY NEGLIGENT IN
FOLLOWING PROPER MAINTENANCE
PROCEDURES. IF YOU FEEL THESE
CHARGES HAVE BEEN ISSUED IN ERROR,
YOU MAY CONTACT THE DEPARTMENT
OF SANITATION, WHO'S MOBILE OFFICE
VISITS CURBSIDE ON TUESDAYS.

THIS VIOLATION INCLUDES, BUT IS NOT
LIMITED TO:
SECTION *OY*1: DUST
SECTION HMM4: IS THAT A MIRROR?
SECTION ERR7: ATTENTION NEEDED TO
POWDERROOM
SECTION NU47: BLATANT DISREGARD OF
PROPER PAPERWORK
SECTION EEK8: LEAVES, DIRT, AND AS-
SORTED SPIDER PARTS ON FLOOR.

**YOU HAVE 24 HOURS TO MAKE THE NEC-
ESSARY CORRECTIONS, OR RISK HAVING
ABOVE IDENTIFIED FACILITY REMOVED
BY THE DEPARTMENT OF SANITATION
THE TUESDAY FOLLOWING THIS CITA-
TION. THE DEPARTMENT OF SPIDERS
WILL AT THAT TIME FORM A CAUCUS TO
DECIDE WHO WILL TAKE OVER SAID
FACILITY.**

**ISSUING OFFICER: MAMAN
TIME: 23:52 HOURS**

~ ~ ~

That night, there was a victory of light over
darkness and dust, as our small band of men,
armed only with a sponge and a broom, miraculously triumphed.

Now… to stoke all that enthusiasm with the
ultimate opportunity – Passover cleaning.

I took another deep cleansing breath, and
grabbed a leftover Purim treat for support.

That's it! Purim! Adar! How could I have
missed it! There is a special commandment to
be joyful in Adar, the month on the Jewish calendar when Purim is celebrated – which is also
the month when most of our Passover preparations are done. Hashem did not put Adar, with
its booster pack of joy and calories, thirty days

before Passover by accident – NO – He is giving us instruction: "When we annihilate the *chametz* do so with sea-splitting joy!" Clean out all that leavened food with *chayus* – zest!

If those women could convince their dispirited downtrodden husbands to bring children into a world devoid of light and hope, then surely we can get the crew to schlep a few boxes and peel a few potatoes. We are those women. We can do this! …We'll enchant with song and dance… use some flowery language…we will do whatever it takes to reach the ultimate goal – preparing Passover while creating traditions our children will yearn to pass on to the next generations. Traditions of joy.

I clutched my image of those fabulous women – the very women this holiday celebrates and I must become. I dug out my tambourine, my clown nose, and a few not too stale Purim truffles for added support. I turned on some music, danced a few measures, and got back to work. I'll breathe later.

~ ~ ~

BS'D

With Gratitude to Hashem,
Please join us
Sunday 11th of Adar
As we Celebrate the

Opening Day of
Passover Cleaning!

Morning Prayers will begin at 10:00 am
Followed by a decadent breakfast.
The windows will be open
with that *fantastic* scent in the air.
There will be lively music,
accompanied by the vacuum,
with spray bottles and
shmattas of all colors and shapes,
and a Fancy overpriced kosher for Passover Cake
For crossing the finish line!

R.S.V.P. Maman and Daddy

Driven by Faith

H aving been dowsed with gasoline, I stood there dizzy, shivering from cold and fumes, shocked by what had just happened to me..

I looked my assailant in the eyes, revealing my distress and bewilderment. She stared back at me, her hand now on the trigger, as she struggled with her emotions – disbelief at what she had just done, confusion as to what she would do next.

Slowly, her composure began to crumble. It began with a slight quiver of her lip, a tear forming in her eye... and then, without warning, a torrent of nervous energy came pouring out in cries of … hysterical laughter.

Her accomplice – an identical twin sister – was behind the wheel of the old van, slapping the dashboard and howling with laughter at the sight of her sister's first lesson in pumping gasoline.

My instruction: "…You need to release the nozzle before youuuuu …" was incomprehensible at the speed the enthusiastic teen was moving.

While smoke ribbons rose off my gasoline-drenched clothing now airing on the porch, the family was briefed concerning the curious odor overpowering the house, along with the day's driving lesson mishaps. Their brother sat shaking his head lovingly as only an older brother can.

Some people seek spiritual highs by bungee jumping or hang gliding off a cliff. Others run with the bulls. If you are searching for the ultimate spiritual adventure – have a child. Not big enough? Have a bunch of them. But if you want to reach the zenith – the ultimate revelation of faith – teach those children to drive.

More daring than allowing them to juggle torches; more courageous than chaperoning field trips to the aquarium and retrieving papers from the piranha tank – don't ask– more fearless than even allowing the baby of the family to go off to kindergarten, *this* is the greatest test of our bitachon, our pure faith.

Nothing compares to the level of fear and faith I have cultivated buckled to the edge of my seat in our big old beat up red 15 passenger van – our sole vehicle. A goliath of a van that appears to its passengers not only to be driving in both lanes, but lapping over the sidewalks, threatening to collect side mirrors off innocently parked cars. This skewed perception is such a frightening phenomenon that my husband still yelps when subjected to a ride in the passenger seat. That we have managed not to pull the door in past its frame is a testament to how well these old vans are made.

All the near misses while merging, all the cars almost backed into, the bumps in our doors, and side mirrors we have broken off will all someday be placed on a great scale when we are asked what acts of pure faith we have performed in our lifetime.

One son, with the ink still drying on his permit, jumped right up into the van, gagged the starter, roared the V8 engine, and then slammed the brake. How he escaped flipping the back end over the front of this behemoth is something Hashem must still be cleaning up from. And he is in good company with other siblings who have performed this stunt in front of the Department of Motor Vehicles. Why they even allow their younger siblings to enter the building for permit tests is still a mystery to me.

But they do. So, I have rolled down hills... backwards... screaming, while a daughter sorted out which pedal was the brake, and which gear was drive. And nothing was as bonding as idling in a busy intersection, with a bus heading towards me, while at the wheel sat my daughter – frozen in fear. No, there's nothing like pondering life and death together, two or three times a day, to bring out the closeness in your relationship – with your children, and with G-d.

I have learned that with a few chapters of Psalms, and a dab of rescue remedy behind each ear, I can survive the time it takes to drive home across the bridge with no oxygen to my brain or blood to my knuckles. But I have also learned to breathe that length of bridge... and to smile... and sometimes, I even sing. I resist the urge to close my eyes, and although I do keep a small hammer/knife gadget in the glove box, I have even stopped planning out worst-case scenarios of dramatic underwater escapes. No. This is the moment when I show my children that I have faith that they are ready to take the driver's seat in their own lives. Faith that, no matter what, G-d will be right there with them. Even if He is silently screaming along with their mother.

As each child goes to take his driver's test, I sit in the little parent hand-wringing room, with a prayer book in mine. I speak to Hashem, "You know that if it were up to me I would bubble wrap and store him safely in the house where the sun and other hazards would never get to him. We have done our part to prepare him well – he has passed all of our tests of skill and maturity – this one is Yours. Hashem... make it good for him, safe for him, and allow him to pass with confidence. And if it would not be good, heaven forbid, please don't let him pass. I beg of you to continue riding alongside him, no matter how frightening it may appear. Hashem... You are in charge."

Distracted one time, I realized only a few minutes before my son and his examiner was due to arrive back that I had not yet done my part. I began my conversation with Hashem with vigor. Moments later, they arrived back – neither one looking particularly cheerful.

We began the ride home in silence – "I don't know what happened!?", "I was doing so well until the last minute when I got *all* these points taken off and failed!" I waited until he got his license to apologize and admit my crime.

Gratefully, we now have a nice corps of very capable 15 passenger van drivers who are deployed when called upon by camps and communities. However, we are not even half way through the license chapter. We will need to evaluate how much longer both the old van and I will last at this.

Although still known to yelp and hold my breath, I have witnessed more miracles than the Jews in the desert, watching Hashem protect and take care of us literally from His passenger seat. My faith has grown more solid than the steel on the old van. However, the fifteen, as she is affectionately called, is not fairing as well. She needs her gas tank tapped with a hammer to get her going, she's on her second set of side-view mirrors, and she no longer has air. Actually, that's not true. She has a constant stream of *hot* air; thus, we drive with the windows open and all that praying and screaming is no longer a private matter.

With all the carting of children to and from yeshivahs; all the mitzvot she has taken us to perform, all the praying from passengers and oncoming motorists, all the kindness extended to us by always giving us right of way – "Please, you go first" – we will one day soon need to re-tire our beloved seven-thousand seven-hundred pounds of rusted steel to that sacred place where items used for holy purposes are buried when they are finished being used.

We have calculated that with the old van running somewhere between miles-per-gallon and gallons-per-mile, it might be cheaper to sign the remaining children up for drivers Ed. And miss all of those opportunities to bond with our children? And all those moments to build our faith ever stronger?

Never.

Grab that permit, and a hammer, and I'll pull the fifteen around the corner.

… Do you think she would notice if I slip a bike helmet underneath my hair covering?

Love in a Vacuum

I once gave a blessing to a friend that she should be married for so long that all of the handles should fall off of her pots and pans, as they are gratefully falling off ours. Although truthfully, we haven't been married for nearly as long as the pots and pans would have you believe.

Our family boldly takes household appliances where no equipment has gone before, or was ever meant to go. We once wore out, in six months, a floor that came with a ten year warranty. Unlike the unhandled pots, for which we have perfected the sport of using with multiple potholders, when it comes to vacuum cleaners we usually need to replace them every year or two. This means that we often have the most recent model of whatever is presently on the market. Our new vacuum has a dust container that creates a small tornado when it is on. This lets us know we are truly tearing up the place.

I decided that before the holidays, I would give the house one of those really great vacuuming jobs. You know, where you get into and under every surface, actually attaching the edging gear and all. I lugged the machine up to the top floor and fired her up. Although it was leaving those wonderful "just vacuumed" marks, it just didn't produce quite the sparkle I had expected. I pulled out the attachment hose and felt the strong suction. However, looking through the clear dust container, I noticed that there was no tornado. Not even a breeze. I took the filters out, banged them on the bricks outside, (heaven forbid I should actually go out and buy new ones) and put them back in. This worked well the last time the vacuum stopped picking up. Still no tornado in the dust bucket. Hmmm. Upon further examination, I located the problem. The short hose that began at the brushes and went into the body of the machine was clogged. I got to work.

I unplugged my trusted friend, laid her back so her breathing passage was unobstructed and started pulling stuff out of her trachea with my fingers. Amazing how much was in there! When my fingers could no longer reach the clog, I grabbed a crochet needle. Perfect tool for the job. Although the pile on the floor was quite impressive, there was no light coming through yet. When my crochet needle could no longer reach the obstruction, I found a kid-sized pool cue. With a few stabs, I had her cleared and an even more impressive pile on my carpet. I looked down into the tube, and saw what was likely the instigator of the problem. There was a large sewing needle stuck in the hose and lying across the opening. Likely, most things were able to go past it, until one piece got stuck. Then other things got backed up behind that piece. Slowly, the amount that got stuck increased, while the volume that could pass through decreased. Although it was still leaving those just-vacuumed tracks, almost nothing was passing through.

We had all been commenting to the child whose job it is to vacuum, "Are you sure you remembered to do this room?" With the pace of life being what it is, we never thought to check the vacuum. I wonder just how long it had been clogged and not picking up. And how long had that needle been in there? I took some pliers and gently removed the needle. I cleaned off the brush roller, started her up, and did that torna-do whirl!

But life doesn't happen in a vacuum. Or maybe, sometimes it does.

Sometimes, in any type of relationship, a blockage can occur. A hurt. A place where someone is not heard or validated, or perhaps their trust or honor is broken. Although we may try to get past the hurt, sometimes it just gets stuck there, blocking the flow of our relationship in a minimal and sometimes unperceived way. We can go on managing just fine, but other things are getting stuck on that hurt. Some of these may otherwise not even bother us. If we ask for help, a friend may look at us as if to say, "Come on, can't you just let that one go?" We can't seem to, though. The little voice of our evil inclination convinces us that the offense is connected to the original hurt and that makes it important to hold onto.

We continue gathering more "stuff": misunderstandings, oversensitivity, intolerance. These obstruct the flow of giving, bringing distance in the relationship. The noise from not feeling connected hums in the background of our day. We start to get that tired feeling; the enthusiasm is gone. We may all of a sudden notice that although things are still functional – we are, after all, still leaving those "just vacuumed" tracks – time together is… well, not quite what we have grown to expect or desire.

We may then try to reboot the relationship in ways that have worked before. But for some reason they don't do it this time. We just can't seem to get back in touch with the emotions we know we have – or once had. Those strong feelings of connection are not felt. When this has been going on for a while, you may hear someone say, "It will never go back to the way it was." Sometimes, sadly, they may say, "It was never really good," not able to remember or believe how truly powerful and delightful this relationship once was.

What can we do?

We need to stop and give some thought to where the blockage occurred. What was the hurt – the piece that we have not been able to get past or bounce back from? When was it that the healthy need to give, connect and get closer started to shut down? Once the source of the problem is identified, it can, with some effort, be removed, and the flow of peace and blessings restored.

Once the light in your relationship is again shining through, you will be able to see your connection with your friend/parent/child/sibling/spouse again. It is also likely that you will appreciate that bond more than ever before – when done properly, a good cleaning out can leave us feeling closer. In fact you may wonder how all of those small things could have ever

bothered you so much. Now they flow peacefully by.

I will leave you a blessing that you should be
married for so long that all of the handles
should fall off your pots and pans, *and* the tornado should never cease to fly in all of your
cherished relationships.

My Part of the Bargain

J ust a few more strokes of mascara and I'm ready to go! It is roughly 5am. The weather looks great for the long drive. Bedding, socks and plenty of books were all packed. While making the appropriately odd facial expression in the mirror, I hear my son in his little sister's bedroom next door:

"Wake up. I am going away to *yeshivah*" – the next level of religious school learning.

I feel a pang in my heart. I close my mouth and put down the wand. The mascara will be useless. How could I have forgotten about this part?

She is cuddled safely in her bed, curls tossed about, still warm and sleeping and absolutely unaware that something precious in her life is about to be taken away from her. He is her adoring older brother, who is always there for her. From here forward there will be a brief visit home for holidays, and then off to yeshivah, until the next break. Then off to camp, and back again to yeshivah.

The youngest brother is standing in the front room in the dark, staring out the window. He has his older brother's oversized black hat balancing on his small ears. I see the sobbing from his back and hear his quiet cries. I wake another sibling to sit and comfort him. The most cherished person in his world is going away.

What was I thinking? When I said I could drive the boys to yeshivah, I merely calculated the number of hours it would take and the responsibilities that needed to be taken care of while I was away. I arranged for each child to take over a piece of my day: one in charge of morning prayers and breakfast, another in charge of lunch. Another to drive the youngest to a party, and one to get the girls to school. Another for an activity, one to wake everyone else, and one to run family clean up. It would be a great experience for the children – sure, I can drive them. Everything is in place! Everything except... my heart. I forgot about this part and now I am driving down the highway, wiping tears, and petitioning Hashem to help me keep it together.

I look at them in my rearview mirror. An older brother returning for another year, and another one going for the first time, both asleep in the back seat. I look at that new one who's leaving. He looks so vulnerable. Can it really be the end of my job? Having already sent a few boys away, I am experienced enough to know it is not really over. They usually call within the hour.

No, the job isn't done. I will still be advising, nurturing, troubleshooting, watching his challenges, praying for him and worrying about him.

But there is something that is over. I look at him and want to apologize to him for being impatient that time in the kitchen when he was just a little guy. And apologize to Hashem for not appreciating enough the totally adorable son He gave me. I wish I had taught him "this" better, and worked with him on "that" some more. I see why it's usually the dads who drop them off... this is not a mom thing to do! How could I have forgotten?

We avoided sending our first son away with all that we had. We moved away from where life worked to go to a new city, so that we could continue to be a family through middle school. Two years later when he graduated high school early, it could no longer be postponed. We all stood at the train platform, a bawling crowd of brothers and sisters, absolutely falling apart with emotion. Okay, so I wasn't much better. I think the people on the train watching us were even crying... "What forsaken place has this young man been exiled to?" Truth was, he would be coming back in a few weeks for Yom Kippur. What a scene we made!

During the weeks that followed, I walked around spontaneously crying. We all seemed to be grieving in a way. It was the end of an era where it was always all of us together. Did I give him all that he needed to go out there? My mentor told me clearly no, which I curiously found very comforting. It is just not possible for any of us to do that.

I see my oldest now, tall with broad shoulders, a beautiful beard (which only seems to grow if you send them away – although I have noticed that sideburns need small excursions home to make their appearance). And those eyes. When he was born, I remember how those eyes intimidated me with their depth and look of wisdom. His eyes now shine with kindness, warmth, beauty, his hurts, his experience, and all the beautiful learning that has been poured into them. And there is something there that I could never have given to him. Something only a bed away from home, a devoted rabbi and a group of other young men could have brought out in him.

With the next son, also now with a small beard, the tears started to flow as he practiced his graduation speech for me in the basement. I can still see it. But the strength he came back with from his years away... amazing, *Baruch Hashem!* I go to synagogue when they are home, just to gaze and admire these men of ours standing with my husband on the other side of the curtain.

I know this one will grow too. I know he, too, will be fine. Okay, I can't possibly convince myself at this moment. If I don't, though, I will need to pull over.

This is so crazy... so wonderful yet so painful. Yes, Hashem, You know this is what I have prayed for over those Sabbath candles I light each Friday night. It's not that I don't appreciate this moment with all my heart. I am truly grateful! But isn't it my privilege to cry? It's like labor; it's wonderful, *and* it hurts. It's just higher up, in my chest. In my heart and soul. Something is shifting. He is going on to his own life now. It is about him and his life's adventure. Truth is, it always was.

I have only good things to look forward to. His strength, his beard, another knowledgeable rabbi in the house,... grandchildren! But for now, I am grieving.

Hashem, please help me keep it together long enough to say a respectable goodbye. Help me find my sense of humor! Come on please! Help me remember not to volunteer to do this again in two years when the next son goes. *Oy* please help us pay for it! Remind me not to go into the dorm or cafeteria... no decent mother would ever leave her child in such conditions. Hashem please protect him, and all the other sons whose mothers are home... crying.

There have been many more teary eyed goodbyes since then. Many more mornings where an older brother has woken a younger sibling with those painful words, "Wake up. I am going to yeshivah." One child used to point and say her brother's name each time we passed the bus station, believing with all her heart that he lived there. Goodbyes at airports for community service. Goodbyes for what would sometimes be almost a year's time as we have sent these boys off, giving them over, but holding on tightly with our hearts.

This past year I had the pleasure of *being* driven to yeshivah by one of our sons. We talked, listened to music and lectures, enjoyed a rest stop together. We said goodbye, both looking into each other's eyes. Both of us smiling. He, knowing he would be back home in a couple weeks. Me, knowing how strong and beautiful he would return, with broadened shoulders and the beginnings of a beard, and that light and strength shining from his eyes. A strength that he needed from having his socks, books and bedding away from home. And we were both okay.

Now...I am wondering if anyone can tell me how to possibly send away twin girls.

Cooked to Non-perfection

"**Y**our mother is eating like a horse."
My husband spoke with such pride and enthusiasm to our daughter who was calling home from camp.

"Is Maman still doing that macrobiotic thing?" she asked.

"Yes... she just ate a whole bowl of millet and seeds. I'm so proud of her."

As I watched for signs that the miso in my pot of soup was miso-ing, I found his pride both uplifting and encouraging. He knew that finding a love of cooking had been a journey for me – one that I was still traveling on.

My husband loves cooking and is fabulous at it: I am awed watching him as he lifts pot covers to experience the bouquet, choosing just the right spices, blending the aromas and sensations like a perfectly danced waltz. I, on the other hand, can finish eating a meal, only learning that it is spoiled when he walks through the door and asks "What *is* that smell?" With little sense of smell and taste, I am a delightful guest, but not a great cook.

As a newly married wife, I wanted so much to cook something special for my new husband. Never having cooked much before, I found an old copy of Gourmet Magazine, with a recipe for ratatouille – a dish I had heard him speak of with great pleasure from his childhood in France – and gave it a try. The list of spices was extensive, and directions highly detailed. I scanned my spice rack: I did not have all of the spices the recipe called for, and certainly not any fresh spices. Fresh spices, dried spices – could there really be such a difference? I measured cups of dried spices to replace the fresh ones in the recipe and although my ratatouille looked more like fresh-cut grass than the dish in the photo, it made a homey and rather spicy smell in our apartment.

Next, I found a recipe for a pear tart, and a flan to round out the meal. More childhood favorites. Again the magazine was big on details and I did my best to follow with my limited knowledge and resources. The flan never came out – the dish sunk to the bottom of the pan of water it was to float in to cook evenly. The tart however cooked evenly – it was breathing up and down as I removed it from the oven – evenly charred. Ever polite, my husband tasted the ratatouille and smiled at me through wet appreciative eyes. My husband did the cooking for the next 11 years.

Until…

One day, perhaps as a reaction to eating something spoiled, I had an epiphany: If at those times in a Jewish marriage when physical intimacy is not appropriate a woman does not serve food directly to her husband, then there must be something powerful in a wife serving her husband food.

I remembered stories of those women in Egypt, who would go out into the fields where their husband had collapsed, exhausted from slave labor and broken spirit. These women would bring food to their husbands, renewing their faith, giving them the will to live and even to bring children into the world.

Food definitely had a power to it and I was not going to miss out on anything that could bring strength to our marriage. I needed to learn how to cook.

I called a mentor. I explained the sorry state of my culinary limitations, and my strong desire to support my marriage. She gave me a blessing and a few simple recipes to start with. "You can do this", she assured me. And I did.

My meals were not necessarily *not* to die for – they were simple, nutritionally balanced and tasty. My husband appreciated both the effort and, gratefully, the food. In fact, I was becoming a proficient cook, with that special power to connect stirred right into my meals.

As life got busier, I managed to keep the dance in my kitchen going with happy meals lovingly cooked and served. I still had my mishaps; like the rushed morning I stood offering my son oatmeal, wearing a large brown circle across the center of my lavender robe where the flames had shot out from under the pot. "I made it special…." But I had achieved the goal and had many happy customers.

Until….

One day, feeling a bit over cooked, I went to visit a natural practitioner. Her suggestion: "You need to nurture yourself more. The macrobiotic diet with its neutral pH and meditative preparation style is just the ticket." She explained what this entailed. I wondered if it wasn't the ticket to the other side of sanity for an already busy woman who had a delicate relationship with being in the kitchen in the first place, but I took her cookbook and dove in.

As I dealt with my busy morning: getting children off to yeshivah, calling the passport office, the US Senators office, and the airlines, I stirred my pots, yielding smoked millet, toasted barley, and charred browned rice. I burned my arm, I burned my fingers, I set my cookbook on fire while cooking with one hand, while its blistered companion soaked sorrowfully in a bowl of cool water. I needed help.

I found a kosher macrobiotic caterer near my home where I donned an apron and learned how to cut vegetables. The chefs were kind, skilled and devoted: "Start from the top of the vegetable, cutting on an angle, thinner, no, thinner, layering it like so, with a little bit of seaweed." It was frighteningly detailed, and I wondered quietly if G-d really would bring healing through a vegetable that when soaked in water resembled an octopus?

After 2 days of slicing, I produced my first edible soup.

And after 4 weeks, I hit ground zero.

I had not tasted anything yummy in a month, I dreaded greeting those pots each day, and even worse – once I finished, I still needed to cook something the rest of the family would want to eat. My determination was waning. I emailed my practitioner:

"When we met, you found me dangerously balancing on the edge. I must tell you that I am now holding onto a root vegetable dangling precariously over that cliff. All those details!! I feel deprived and miserable. If this is about the energy I am putting into my food, then my amaranth will surely combust on contact. With my swollen belly I feel like Gandhi – except with chubbier legs, more clothing, and no peaceful smile."

She responded, "You sound good. You have the strength to complain."

I sounded good?

I missed that carefree girl who worked with my husband on the car, privately enjoying heaping spoonfuls of cookies and cream ice cream with each trip I made to retrieve a tool from the house. He was so impressed as he looked into the nearly empty half gallon container that was purchased the night before… "I've *never* seen *anyone* do that."

And where was the girl that he busted power walking on the treadmill, with the bag of potato chips from his desk now tucked under her arm?

Most of all, I missed that happy woman who had worked so hard to create that special power to bring connection in her marriage, bringing joy, peace and blessing to our home. And I imagine everyone else did too.

Hearing pots clanging and my sorry mumbling, my son came into the kitchen. "What's going on in here!?"

That tall, kind young man, who cooks for hundreds of children and staff at camp each summer, looked into my eyes with gentle concern and compassion as I described the biology-slide-like-onion-cutting and other atrocities. "I can help", he said.

I pulled up a kitchen stool and watched as he stood quietly slicing and dicing daikon radishes, carrots and onions. I found myself comforted by his help, soothed by his calm, and lulled by the rhythm of his cutting. I took a deep cleansing breath; so this is what it was supposed to look like.

Beautiful piles of colorful micro-cut vegetables began to appear. The macrobiotic preparation may be serene and meditative for someone who enjoys cooking and is on vacation with nothing on his plate, but my life has many plates that are each filled with meaningful and wonderful things. My dance resembles more the woman at the circus who spins plates on top of dowels, running back and forth, giving each dish momentum as it wobbles or loses its balance.

Even to my unsophisticated nose, something about all this smelled mildly familiar. Wasn't this the same voice of the evil inclination that I had heard years ago singing: "Impress your new husband with some fancy recipes?" And wasn't it the voice of reason, with her blessing and simple advice that helped me create that special strength I so wanted in my marriage?

It is G-d who gives the power of healing to a doctor, to a medication, and even to seaweed if He decides to do so. It was also G-d who caused the fish to swim into the vessels the women in Egypt brought with them to draw water, giving them food they could cook and serve to their husbands. Shalom, peace, is the vessel that blessings are collected in, and there is no stronger vessel to draw down blessing than the shalom between husband and wife. Where there is shalom, that's where G-d wants to be, and I was not going to chase Him out of my kitchen with tension over slicing and dicing, destroying the peace I had created with cooking to bring Him there in the first place.

Balance is an ingredient I often forget to throw in to what I am brewing, both in the fresh and dried versions, but it is certainly one I can work on using more often. I could start with simple additions to my present dance, allowing each new skill to simmer until comfortable, and then add something new. It will be a sort-of-macrobiotic diet, with a more laid-back preparation style with a unique smoked quality to it, and that special power to connect stirred right in. I need only do my best, and Hashem will add the blessing.

As I watched the miso in my pot finally misoing, I breathed deeply. Yes, it had been a long journey. But there was strength and shalom.

Shalom for husband and wife.

Shalom for wife and kitchen.

Just the Two of Us

T he house was still vibrating.

The last child had left, pulling behind her the last semi-rolling duffel with her brothers' leather belts supporting its girth. Inside her hipsterish-looking bag she packed the remaining camp towels – tossing the one we shook out to discover a terrycloth frame with the two of us looking through at each other, crying with laughter, as only camp packing at 2am can do.

Since the birth of our first child, this was the first time the stars had aligned leaving my husband and I the only ones at home. The oldest

three were now married, the next one in New
York, the twins touring Israel and Europe, another in Sydney, and the youngest two off at
camp.

Even the opossum had packed out.

"Why didn't you tell someone when you saw
an opossum go upstairs?"

"Oh Maman, you should have seen how cute
he looked – first he pulled his front end up a
step and then wiggled his back half to join it,
then stretched his little feet to the next step...."
The two sisters gushed in agreement.

"Can't you just scream like regular girls? He
scared me silly in the hallway."

The grey headed rat like creature was pacing
back and forth outside the twins bedroom, confirming both of our suspicions – there was
snacking going on in there. My chivalrous husband heard my gasp, got up and chased the
opossum downstairs where he took up residence under the bookcase, appearing nightly to
flash his shark-like smile.

"Isn't he sweet looking?" I must have missed
something.

Our opossum must have been lonely for the
liveliness of our nighttime crew who wrote
books and papers, built computer games, and
booked rooms in castles throughout Europe,
while they created incredibly aromatic snacks
throughout the night. When my neighbor re-

ported finding an opossum in her garbage, "…really Faig, no kidding?" I realized we were actually alone.

I remember contemplating just this scenario with a four year old I had pulled from the tub: "Maman…" she looked up at me with her deeply concerned eyes peeking out from the towel, "…soon I'm going to go to school. And then my brother is going to go to school. And then…" the tears began to fall, "…you're going to be… *all by yourself!*" We held each other and cried – her tears over the sadness of my impeding loneliness, mine from the sensitivity of this magical child. She then looked up hopefully: "I'm going to pray for another baby so you won't be alone." I was soon enjoying the company of another child, my imminent loneliness postponed for a few more years.

But this was no time for sudsy reminiscing. The first child was due back in three weeks, and after an intense year of marrying off three kids, starting a new business and the general chaos of supersized life, we were ready to embrace the opportunity that G-d had moved heaven and earth to create.

We let the children know that this was our time to recharge, reconnect, play, and perhaps enjoy a little quiet. We then made some humble plans – we would breathe deeper, and maybe sit on the couch again. We would finish sentences, and cook small portions of food. We would put aside anything that could wait, clearing the decks for time together in the evenings.

We adventured with the children through their photos and comments posted daily on the family WhatsApp, laughing, missing them, and in awe of all they were doing. We in turn posted our own photos of biking, scouting out new places, feeding potato chips to geese, and long meals with weird healthy foods. We were enjoying that playfulness that came with less apparent obligations. But the quiet... it never really came.

"I was thinking of visiting this Shabbat", came the first phone call from a child looking forward to the opportunity to being just the *three* of us, and feeling a little badly that we were all alone. A sweet and tempting offer.

"Are you guys coming for visitor's day?" came the next call.

There were tummy aches in Europe, advice for couples just settling in, and unscheduled calls home from camp that we needed to monitor our phones for. We would get ready for sleep and someone would need to talk. And when would our new daughter go into labor anyway? It was all the greatest privilege and we loved being wanted, involved and valued. However, alone was getting busier than... not alone.

In an attempt to regain the dream, we posted on the family WhatsApp: Emergencies only. And that's just what we got.

With the baby now arrived, we decided to take a few days away, leaving our not so quiet, quiet home. After some boating, hot dogs, and time spent on Visitor's Day with our son, we set our GPS to our hotel. We were routed north near where we live, and then south again to our destination. We rerouted and got the same directions. We even tried another program but could not get a direct route. Alas.

It was late as we passed near our home and we decided to stay for the night, setting out again in the morning. When I awoke, I found my husband downstairs feeling just not quite right. We decided to stay around and see where it went.

As the day progressed, so did his uncomfortable feeling. "Smile for me", I asked him. Although his crooked smile was charming, a quick call to our doctor confirmed it, "Take him in right away."

My husband was quickly hooked up to tubes and machines. The doctors spoke as they wheeled him out of his room, "We're going to take him for a CT scan, to make sure he's not having a brain bleed."

Oh... a brain bleed. Think good, it will be good. I ran out to the parking lot to get clarity and better reception, and got on the family WhatsApp. I explained the situation to the children as clearly and gently as I could. One by one they answered the plea: "OK, we are splitting up the book of *tehillim*, Psalms. "I've got the first portion, who wants the next?" I watched as the children awoke in their different time zones and got on board with all they had to offer. They posted their father's name on their numerous WhatsApp groups asking for prayers and deeds of kindness in his merit. Letters went to the Ohel pleading for protection. One son found a young man going to his chuppa, while another found a bride to petition the heavens. One child hoping to surprise us was on her way home when she awoke to the news: "I'll be there soon." Those kids were a force to be reckoned with, storming the heavens while calming and comforting, building strength for us both. No, we were really not alone.

With tests reviewed and medications dispensed, we were given the diagnosis: Bell's Palsy, an inflammation of a nerve in the face, a condition that mimics the symptoms of a stroke. He was going to be OK. *Baruch Hashem* – so grateful! We needed to stabilize his vitals before he would be released, but a few weeks of non-inflammatory eating, lower stress, more prayer, and he would be back to himself.

I layered a warmed blanket on my husband, and wrapped myself in one as well. As I took my post at the side of his bed, I listened to the beeps of the sensors, watching his vitals stabilize and his body relax into a deep sleep. I thought about our children, grateful for each one, and all the courageous things they had done to help; the doctors, the nurses, even the GPS that would not allow us to venture too far. I thought about my husband and how grateful I was to have him in my life. We sat this way in the calm and quiet for hours, with feelings of gratitude filling the space.

"It's a shame you and Daddy never got to go away this summer", one child remarked. Our goal for our getaway, and the three weeks we had been gifted, was to clear a space so that we could see each other without distractions, to re-connect to the priority of each other in our lives – to reconnect to one another. What we had not accomplished in three weeks, G-d had arranged to happen in a moment.

"Would you like to join us for dinner?" we offered the child who had come home.

"That's OK. I don't really like steamed beets, carrots, or beans. Mind if I eat at a friend's?"

So once again, it was just the two of us.

Dancing with Light in a Courtroom

What gave the night its special charm? Perhaps it was Fraidle in that crazy moose head and kimono, or Rochel preposterously posing as an electric company representative responding to a "disturbance of the peace" call.

As we all sat in the crowded minivan, parked on the gravel driveway outside the home of our first victim – Miriam, a woman who could be considered the instigator of this insanely wonderful ritual – I explained to the seminary girls how this whole mishugas, this charming craziness, got started.

It all began with a backpack….

As I remember it, I was straightening up after the morning rush hour, when I found an unfamiliar backpack in my front room. The backpack belonged to a young boy who had visited the day before. A boy who deserved a kindness more than a lesson. So, despite the to do lists swirling in my head, I jumped into my big old red 15 passenger van to deliver the backpack to the Yeshivah.

Absorbed in thought, I absentmindedly turned too early, ending up on a street I almost never take. I pulled over to allow a police motorcycle to pass and pursue his target. I soon realized that *I* was his target.

"Ma'am, I clocked you at 26 miles per hour in the school zone. The speed limit in a school zone is 15. License and registration, please."

He took my documents and disappeared behind my old van, leaving me to cringe in the driver's seat at the stares of passerby, and the thought of him writing out my ticket while leaning against the *"Friends Don't Let Friends Drive Junk"* sticker on the back door of my old beat-up van.

"Ma'am, you may want to bring this to court."

"Sir, if you say I was going 26, I have no reason to doubt you."

"Ma'am... you don't understand. This is a *very* serious ticket. Take a look."

The yellow tissue paper testified to the weight of my crime – four points on my license plus $585 in fines.

I went to court.

My day in court arrived. I sat reciting chapters of Psalms, while a bold and confident looking judge dismissed case after case.

"Five unpaid parking tickets... hey, that's no good! What's that all about?" Giving the man a look intended to vaporize him, the judge nevertheless concluded, "Dismissed."

"Driving on the sidewalk." Looking at the next man, shaking his head with a smirk, as if both annoyed and entertained by the *chutzpah*, "...Dismissed."

"Deray!" the clerk called out.

I closed my prayer book and approached the judge's bench. I admitted my guilt, and told the judge that I was grateful for the wakeup call and had been more careful since this incident. I then added that I did not see the sign, and gave him a photo showing how the "School Zone" sign is blocked by the "No Right on Red" sign if you are sitting at the traffic light, which I had been. I told him about the boy, the backpack, and even the fact that it was the first speeding ticket I had ever gotten. The Judge pulled back from his desk, giving his lungs some additional space, and began scolding me as if I were a small child standing in the principal's office. He yelled at me for not obeying the speed limit and lectured me about the harm I could have caused. He threatened that the officer could have taken away my license right there on the spot. He ended off with loud and angry words: "I am not even going to *consider* this case until you do 20 hours of community service! See the clerk!"

I took what was left of my dignity to the desk of a sweet older Southern woman sitting to his right. With apologetic eyes, she softly explained to me that she would reschedule my case to appear at his bench again in three months. I was to bring a signed letter, on letterhead, from an organization of my choice, confirming that I had completed my 20 hours of community service.

Walking outside the courthouse my thoughts swirled. What was that all about? That was… crazy! Undeniably – he was absolutely right! And it was terrifying to think of the possibility of harming a child, heaven forbid. But, I was told these tickets usually get reduced or even dismissed if you go to court. And the change in the judge's posture, and how aggressive he had become with me? What was that all about? I was only there because the police officer told me to go. And I was only doing a kindness when all of this started.

This was not processing in a normal way – the disparities felt too… crazy. My heart lightened. This was not about the judge. This was from Hashem. I think Hashem wants something from me, and it needs to be… just as crazy, I suppose.

All kinds of out of the box ideas came to mind. Crazy colorful wonderful schemes. But the thought that kept floating to the top was something I had recently learned. It was about the women who left Egypt: Even in the darkest moments of that terrible exile, their faith in the Redemption was so strong that they crafted tambourines with which to dance and sing when that day finally arrived. It was in the merit of these women and their faithfulness that we were taken out of Egypt. Today, though, this is not enough. We need to start dancing NOW, even while still in the midst of this this present exile.

Those words touched me deeply. And as I put those words into action, I found that dancing added strength and light to my life. When I would hit an obstacle and felt all my usual resources were exhausted, and I could no longer move a challenge with regular methods, I would dance. I would dance to add joy to my day, or even to warm up a room. One time, I was all by myself, dancing away, my ear buds in and eyes closed, lost in the melody, when I felt an uncomfortable feeling. I opened my eyes to find my husband there, standing like a deer caught in the headlights.

"What are you doing!?" he asked to his supposedly sane and dignified wife. Now looking like two deer caught in the head lights, I countered with, "How long have you been standing there?"

Dancing. Faith. Light. The gears began to turn. I had an idea.

I called my rabbi to arrange to do my community service at the yeshivah, giving me the confidence to know that the 20 hours would be covered in case my crazy plan did not fly.

Then, the idea sprouted legs – multiple ones. I was giving a presentation at a Seminary, and one of the girls asked, "Mrs. Deray, can we do something fun and crazy together? The perfect opportunity! Chanukah was coming. There was no more perfect a time to add more light, more faith… and a little chaos.

One of the girls wrote a beautiful note. We bought flowers, and grabbed our iPods, phones, and speakers for music. Dressed in happy, colorful clothing, we knocked on our first door, and invited the woman of the house into her basement. In between the boxes and pipes, we danced and sang. It was magical! She laughed, danced, shook her head in disbelief, and thanked us profusely. Our spirits soared!

We continued from house to house. Once invited in, we'd steal the woman of the house into a quiet corner, or down into the basement. We evicted husbands and sons. And we danced. Oh, how we danced! We held each other's hands, and we laughed, and cried, and gave each other blessings. We left each woman with a beautiful purple iris, and the note:

This is for every meal you cook, every carpool you drive, every lunch you pack, every tear you wipe away, every heart you mend, and for every spark of light you bring to your family's world. And to ours.

We danced that wonderful night of Chanukah longer than the batteries in our iPods could keep up with, and until there were only a few of us left – exhausted and elated.

Some women called the next day to tell us: "You just don't know what that meant to me,... how much I needed it just at the moment you showed up!" For others it was a knowing smile at the grocery store, or a wink in passing.

How to translate the evening into something I could bring into a courtroom? That was something I would leave up to the wisdom of my rabbi, who would be writing that letter. I prepared and rehearsed my part carefully, knowing what was at stake and that I might have all of about three minutes before the judge might start yelling at me again.

I returned to court to face the judge. Sitting with my Book of Psalms, I watched as a man donned the judge's cloak and took his place. He looked nothing like the judge I thought I was scheduled to see. He was smiling. And he continued with his happy demeanor throughout the morning docket of cases.

"Deray!"

I apprehensively approached the bench. I handed the judge my letter from the rabbi, on Yeshiva Schools letterhead, testifying to my community service – our wonderful evening of dancing and more. I even stapled a copy of the note to the page. The judge carefully inspected the letter, and then looked up at me with a smile.

"Yeshiva Schools. Is that the place over there on Forbes, across from Maxon Towers?"

"Yes."

Now smiling broadly, "I've seen the children leaving from that school. Very impressive! Very impressive place. Do you have a child who goes to that school?"

"Yes. I have a few daughters there. Actually, that's only the girls' school. There is a school for the boys over on Whightman Street. I have some children there too."

"You have how many kids?"

"Nine."

"... Really! Wow, you beat Fitzgerald!"

I was not sure who Fitzgerald was, but he seemed quite excited about it. He continued smiling while he looked back at the letter.

"I've never seen their letterhead before." He silently read the list of officers down the left side of the page. "Very impressive"

He was now looking at the body of the letter, "...dancing with women and bringing them joy...." And he read the note we had given the women. "That's really beautiful.'

Looking up at me curiously, he asked, "You did this?"

"Yes," I nodded.

"That's beautiful." He paused, and then looked at me with sincerity and confusion. "Why did you do this?"

"Well sir, the other judge said that he wouldn't consider my case until I did 20 hours of community service."

"Oh."

...long pause...

Looking at me still with the curious expression he added "This is traffic court. We don't do community service in traffic court."

Uncomfortable, he called over to a clerk, "Hey, Judy... do we do community service in traffic court?"

"No sir."

Looking back at me he said, "Yeah,... we don't do community service in traffic court. But this is very special."

He handed me back my letter with the note stapled to it.

"What are you here for anyway?"

"Well sir, I was going 26mph... in a school zone."

"Oh. Dismissed." "See the clerk."

~ ~ ~

It was raining softly on the van windows as I finished telling the girls the story.

"So that's how this all got started. I still don't know what it was all about. But it was so powerful and so touching... I do it each year. And it's wonderful to have you all along, to dress up in costumes and add your own special talents and chayus, your own over-the-top joyful quality."

And it truly was. This new group of Seminary girls had their own gifts to add to this crazy wonderful mishugas! In addition to dancing with the women, that night we crashed a sleepover party and a class get-together. They gave these younger girls some fun and inspiration as they ad-libbed hilarious pranks at the door, and danced around the room, singing and laughing with them.

I will probably never know what the whole backpack / traffic ticket story was all about, but I have learned that there is a Divine Presence, a Master of the world who choreographs everything. Although from our vantage point, we may only see random chaos, we must always know that there is a G-d who runs the world and pays attention to what we do.

And just a warning: If you are ever in Pittsburgh during the week of Chanukah, be careful when you answer the door after dark.

Making Space for More

"It's time to go."
My husband spoke in a gentle voice.

"It can't be..." I answered, slightly flustered, "there are still three opened boxes of Cheerios that need to be consolidated. And I'm not finished organizing the giftwrap... or the medicine cabinet."

What is it about welcoming children into the family that creates a fever in a woman for order and completion?

I remember being rounder than I thought my body could possibly inflate to, waiting for our jumbo sized twins to arrive. With our photos

organized neatly into albums and the Legos separated from the Duplos, it was now time to take nesting to the next level – I would get the car inspected. Once the twins arrived that would make for six children, the oldest being six. I figured it would be a while before that errand would look important. I pulled the minivan into the gas station and rolled down the window:

"No problem ma'am, just take her over to the garage and pop the hood" the attendant instructed.

After numerous, rather ungraceful attempts to reach further than the twins would allow, I asked him: "Sir, do you think that you could... pull the hood release for me." Shooting me a quizzical look, he opened my car door and stood there staring, "Lady! You look like you're about to explode!"

As I reminisced, my husband looked on with concern while I sorted flat sheets from cornered sheets from pillowcases from – "Sweetie, you can do all of that when we get back. Now, go and get your things. It's time."

Feeling queasy and a little unbalanced, I counted on my husband's strength and clarity – I was too filled with emotion to think clearly. He however was an experienced father, and better than me at knowing when it was time to go. Like the night I underestimated the long ride to the city hospital: As we sped through the empty Boston streets in our big old 15 passenger van, I laid over the seat like a beached walrus, certain that the baby would be born in transit, begging for Hashem to help, and for my husband to run the red lights.

While my husband parked the van, I walked through the deserted hospital atrium, pausing to lay my head on the large planters as the contractions came furiously. The anxious security guard ran over to check on me, "Lady, are you drunk?" As I waved for him to go away, I heard the warm laughter of a nurse coming from the hallway,

"She's not drunk... she's in labor! Here honey...." She hooked her arm through mine and escorted me to the busy labor and delivery desk where the overwhelmed receptionist ordered:

"Ma'am... take a seat."

"But..." She shot me a look that said it all. I sat down, quietly mentioning, "OK... but this is my seventh child."

"SOMEONE GET THIS WOMAN TO A ROOM – NOW!"

This time would be so much smoother. This time we knew exactly when to go. And unlike with the other children, we knew it was going to be a daughter. In fact, we knew her hair color, eye color, and even her sense of humor. This new daughter was coming into our family in a way we had never experienced before. There would be no weight gain, no mad dashes to the hospital, no searching for lost pacifiers or security blankets in the middle of the night. This child had already been raised to adulthood by another mother – a woman who I would forever be indebted to. While I was raising one half of a neshama, a soul, on the east coast, she was raising the other half on the west coast.

"Sweetie, I have the passports and boarding passes… we really need to go now." The time had come for these two halves of a neshama to come together. Hashem was giving us another daughter to love.

Holding a candle in one hand, I laced my arm through this almost-daughter's arm, guiding her as she walked slowly in her lovely white gown, with a veil covering her face. Her mother, my new friend and partner in crime, guided her carefully on the other side. Together we circled our son seven times, creating the spiritual space that would become their home. Each time we passed his face, I drank in the beauty of his sincerity and faith as he asked Hashem to provide them with all that they would need for their lifetime together. As they stood side by side, I watched him shift his center of gravity from "me" to "us", as they asked for health, children and livelihood for all who needed – making full use of the heavens being opened beneath their *chuppa*, the wedding canopy.

The rabbi then called those close to each of them to make blessings. Her mom and I held each other as we watched, laughing and passing tissues, grateful for the privilege of raising these children to this moment, and for the job the other had done with her half of this soul. G-d could have done this any way He wanted to. He could have populated the world with fully grown people who knew all that they needed to know. But instead He gave the job to us very imperfect beings, allowing us the opportunity to love, stumble, and be humbled to depths we never thought possible.

As her father gives a sip of wine to our son, I lift my almost-daughter's veil enough to give her a sip. Although I could never stand in her mother's place, I can love her as a daughter, without a law or a dash to separate us. And I know she will love me – I have raised our son so that she can burn dinner every night bringing familiarity and comfort to her husband's world.

They are reading the *ketubah*, the marriage contract. My part is to love unconditionally whoever our children marry, and to get along with their families no matter what. Like the many facets of a diamond I find our families connect in ways that are familiar, sometimes deep and somewhat wacky.

It is time. I always knew this day would come, and I was determined to love our son fully so that I could give him over completely to his wife. I am sure I missed opportunities, but there are many up ahead – to love them both. Just as we handed him over to a rebbe to guide him in ways that we could not, she is already nurturing hidden strengths within him that only she could bring out. With the ring on her finger, the blessings said and the cup broken, she is now his wife. And our new daughter.

With the week of celebrations now over, I watch as our daughter and son sit in his old room sorting through boxes of childhood treasures. They laugh as he shares stories that make each of the otherwise random items in the eclectic collection invaluable. There is homemade chalk, cards, silly gifts exchanged between siblings, and projects crafted by smaller versions of the same hands now deciding what will be packed and what will no longer be needed. As they sort, organize and start preparing the space for their life together, the sun bounces off the dust they are generating, making them look like a scene in a snow globe. For some reason, it was in that cloud of dust that the transition of lives touched me most.

And we kicked up a lot of dust that year: Two months after flying our family to the west coast to welcome a daughter, and with almost no time for a proper nesting frenzy, we flew the family back to the west coast to welcome another daughter. And 9 months after that, we traveled to the Midwest to welcome the third daughter, in less than a year. Three 20 year old daughters – our first set of triplets, or quintuplets if you add our 20 year old twins. The combined energy of all these *simchas* caused a total purge of the basement, and the timing for that purge could not have been better.

With the Legos once again separated from the Duplos and the cornered sheets sorted out from the flat, the fourth son called,

"Maman, It's time to go." *Baruch Hashem!*

I Leave You with
a Blessing...

May you feel fulfilled, powerful, irreplaceable, and grateful for the privilege to be a partner in creation – the craziest, nuttiest, most unpredictable, meaningful and important job you will ever have. And may you have abundant *nachas* from it – a satisfaction so large that you want to burst out in a song of gratitude, with joy-filled tears running down your face and uninhibited laughter causing those who see you to question your seaworthiness. And may you find this over-the-top joyful quality in endless abundance right in your own home.
I know that you will.

Always know that although the world may

appear to be random chaos, there is a Master of the Universe who choreographs everything, and pays attention to what you do. No matter if you believe in Him or not, He believes in you. Know that you are loved more than you could possibly comprehend. And that your Creator is there for you - unconditionally.

Please be in touch - I love hearing about your successes, enjoy your feedback, and cherish the friendship.

With Love,

Chana Gittle

Chanagittlederay.com

Visit to find out about Classes, Events, Articles, Videos, Blog, and More.

Gratitudes

I am filled with gratitude to Hashem for the opportunity to bring this book to life, and to the many people He sent to join me in the process:

Rivka Bendkia, who added her creative brilliance and energy to this book, bringing a new level of humor and joy with her *Peh* illustrations. I love that we are bringing light into the world together.

Gila Issenberg, my literary agent/"labor coach" and editor who through holidays, weddings, births and my other chaos kept her faith in this project, taking it from an idea I was ignoring to a reality I had no more excuses to not pursue. I am grateful for her expertise, friendship, faith and endless joy.

Alexis Sanders, who added her delightful creative energy, expertise and time to make the covers magical. Gila Issenberg and Devora Deray who carefully edited and edited. The elusive members of the "Brain Trust" for their clarity. Mihal Evan, who made the reproduction of the illustrations really shine. Chaya Mushka Deray, Sara Deray and Raquel Issenberg for their technical assistance. And Adam Issenberg, Charlie Saul, and Rabbi Balin for their kindness and wisdom with legal matters.

The Rebbe, for instructing me to write this book. Rabbi Gavriel Tornek, Rishe Deitsch and Susan Showalter-Bucher – who had the chutzpa to encourage me to fulfill that suggestion. And Reb Jacob Priluck for sending his granddaughter to light the way.

Rivka Goldwasser, who nudged until I submitted the inspirational emails I was writing for a boutique to Rishe Deitch, who published them in The N'shei Chabad Newsletter. Some of the articles in this book were also originally published on Chabad.org, Olam Yehudi and Inyan magazines. I would like to thank these editors and associate editors for making me a part of their beautiful work, and their readership whose feedback and friendship has been such a privilege.

My friends at Sallie Boggs who helped me bridge many worlds, sisters at Woman2Woman Toastmasters, those sparks of light at The Center for Women and PAWW, and Laurie Moser and Deborah Gilboa for their special touch.

Mindy Winston, for the inspiration to make those first basement classes in home management, marriage and parenting skills – this is where it all began. And the beautiful women in Sharon and Pittsburgh who ever inspire me with their determination to fulfill their roles in life with grace and chayus.

The irreplaceable women of valor – my girlfriends, my sisters, who hand in hand laugh, cry and dance as we build lives, weather storms, and raise our families together.

Rabbi and Mrs. Noah Golinkin, Rabbi Hillel and Chani Baron, Rabbi Yitzchok and Zeesy Raskin, The Jacobs Family, Rabbi Chaim and Sara Wolosow, Rabbi Menachem and Chana Gurkow, Rabbi Yankel and Miriam Karp, Rabbi Balin, Mrs. Leah Yehudis Scheiner, The Krakowski family, Rabbi Yisroel and Blumi Rosenfeld, Rabbi Ephriam and Miriam Rosenblum and their family – our Shluchim, for being our role models, teachers, friends, family and beyond. And to the rabbis, morahs and teachers who have guided our children, we are forever grateful.

The Rebbe, for reaching out to our family and changing our lives forever.

My parents, and my husband's parents, who we can never possibly repay, for... *everything*. And all of our siblings for their love.

Our small Jewish nation, who have my husband's kindness and my big feet, and some with smaller feet because they came to us through other parents - they have filled our lives and the pages of this book with joy and chayus, a passion to live by Hashem's laws with a crazy over-the-top joy and humor. I am grateful for their permission to share their stories to bring laughter, hope and courage to others.

And that man on one knee, for his belief in me and for his support, but most of all for being my partner on this crazy wonderful journey.

Made in the USA
Columbia, SC
06 February 2018